THE NAKED DRAFTSMAN

Life Drawing, Nudity and the Function of Clothing

Maurice Cowley

i

About the author

Maurice Cowley was born 21 June 1942 in Sussex. After completing his National Service he spent his working life as a lecturer in, and later a professor of, Mathematics at a well-known university, which he prefers not to name to save that establishment having to acknowledge having condoned his strange interests.

When he retired he was encouraged to take up life drawing and wrote, and illustrated, this little book about his experiences.

THE NAKED DRAFTSMAN

Life Drawing, Nudity and the Function of Clothing

By

MAURICE COWLEY

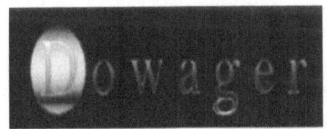

Published by:
DOWAGER BOOKS
www.dowager.com

Dedicated to
Richard Feynman - Physicist, Philosopher, Thinker,
Bongo Player and extraordinary exemplar of the Art
of Life Drawing

Acknowledgements

I would like to thank the university which employed me for so many years and then helped me find a hobby in retirement.

I am also indebted to artists Deborah Swift and Maureen Haskle who have been my colleagues, teachers, models and voyeurs on this journey far beyond my traditional bounds of comfort.

Prof Austy Sheerline and Mrs Alice Measham were stanch supporters during my early student-hood.

Finally I would like to thank my good friend and mentor, the Revd Jowett Javlin for encouraging me to write down my experiences whilst coming to terms with both my humanity and my mortality.

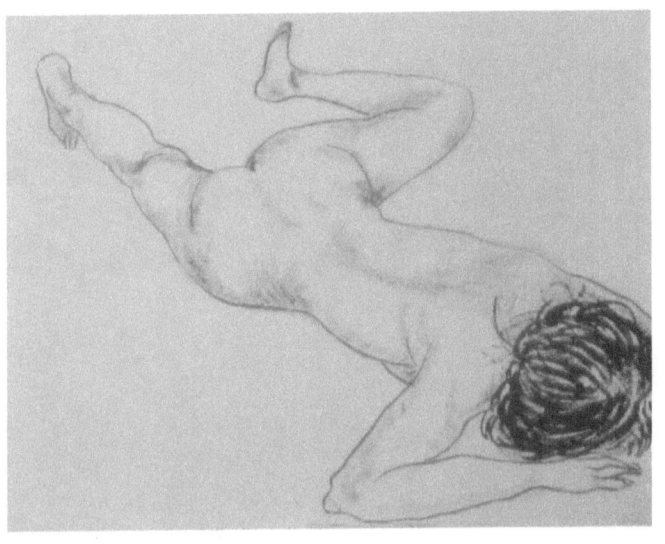

Contents

Prologue - The Wasp and Teapot

Once upon a time, on a warm afternoon in late summer, the drone of insect wings added to the soporific atmosphere in the small sunlit garden by the river side. A wasp was minding its own business as it searched for suitable food for the hungry larva waiting in its nest. To and fro it zoomed its antennae twitching as it searched for traces of the juices of wind-fall fruits or the body fluids of inferior insects it could sting, kill and excoriate.

The river rippled softly in the distance, the sun warmed the wasp's body as it sensed the wafts of sugary strawberries. All felt well in this best of all possible worlds. A warm day, a choice of damsel flies to sting, paralyze and suck out, or a feast of fallen festering strawberries to simply wallow in. What should it do for the best? The damsel flies would try to escape and need chasing and subduing. The strawberries would simply lie in the sun to be devoured. So it made its fateful and inappropriate choice. The strawberries it would be.

It had not been misled by the scent. The *pourri* of strawberries and sugar was rich in nutrients, the wasp darted in to hover above the sickly sweet redness and survey its impending feast. A passing cloud wafted air across the banquet blowing the wasp sideways. It darted back through the turbulent air currents to take up station once more and lower its proboscis into the concentrated nourishment. But the cloud kept wafting it sideways. The wasp was determined and tenacious. The nest needed nourishment, mushy strawberries were an ideal foodstuff and the wasp thought it understood the rules. Fallen, fermented fruit was the easy low risk choice to win it acclaim back at the nest. It fought the turbulence, circled its meal and landed by the edge of the heap. A moment later it was crushed by a hot metal teapot.

It was only when the teapot struck it from above that the consequences of its misunderstanding of its world became apparent. At that moment its choice of alternative life styles ceased, its range of possible futures dwindled to zero as the scope of its soul collapsed beneath the previously unobserved form of a teapot which crushed it against the side of the dish of jam.

It was a human being, taking afternoon tea by the riverbank, who had really understood the full range of possibilities available. All her attempts to brush the wasp away from the jam pot had failed. So she crushed it with the teapot. Had the wasp recognised the possible consequences associated with its choices it could have feasted on damsel flies all day without let or hindrance.

The moral of this tale is that there are dire consequences to making choices if you do not fully understand the world you live in. Some humans have minds which can be trained to perceive what the real choices are and so avoid being crushed by a threatening teapot. This little book describes the attempts of a retired mathematician to increase his understanding of his choices when the world in which he lived began to changes in ways he was not sure he could adapt to.

For forty years he had existed, and thrived, in a world where everything could be explained by the careful application of mathematical symbols and equations. It was a world he understood. Then, at the age of sixty as the hovering teapot of retirement loomed above him. He was sent by his university on a pre-retirement course where he learned that once he stopped attending the university, where he had spent most of his sheltered life, he would need a new focus for his life. A hobby was suggested.

'A hobby?' he had said. 'I've never had a hobby. I wouldn't know where to start.'

'You need a hobby that will get you out of the house and give your wife a chance to get things done without you getting under her feet.' the instructor in creative pursuits had replied well understanding the threat of the looming teapot, of which the professor was blissfully unaware.

'Surely she will prefer me to keep her company.' he said.

'What did she say when you announced you were going to retire?' the instructor asked.

'She said, does that mean you won't be going out at all... ever?' He'd replied. 'She sounded very despondent.'

'That's why you need a hobby.' The instructor helpfully went on. 'To get you out of the house and to make sure you don't join the ranks of the Silver Separators.'

'Silver Separators?'

'The husbands whose wives divorce them when they retire, stay at home and drive them mad by never giving the poor women any time on their own.'

The professor opened his iPad, googled 'Silver Separators' and discovered that there had been a 58.92% increase in the number of couples over sixty getting divorced after the husband retired.

'Perhaps I do need a hobby.' He admitted, ruefully. 'But what can I do?'

'What did you do as a boy?' the instructor asked.

'I drew plans for aircraft and then built and flew them.'

'So that's your answer.' The instructor said grasping wildly at that feeble straw of hope. 'Join a drawing class.'

'And how will I find a drawing class?' The professor asked.

'Google - Life Drawing Classes.' The instructor advised. 'Then you'll get to draw naked ladies instead of model planes.'

'Naked ladies? Ladies without clothes?' the professor said.

'Yes. It will keep you out of trouble and keep your wife happy that you're not bothering her.'

I know this is true because I am that professor and this is the story of how I became a full participant in the social theatre of life drawing and learned a new way of life.

I had spent my whole life studying symbols and trying to explain the world and yet I had remained unaware that flittering over the nearby river of life was a whole new realm of shimmering symbols I knew nothing about. They were enticing me away from the strawberry path of indolence and the threat of the great teapot of death which was looming above my unknowing head.

What cajoled me to learn how to draw was a passing mention the instructor made. 'Did you know that Richard Feynman was good at drawing nudes?'

'Richard Feynman, the Nobel Prize winner and father of Quantum Electro Dynamics?'

'Yes.' He used to go out and draw naked ladies to get out from under his wife's feet and he stayed married for the rest of his life.'

'Well that makes it worth considering.' I replied, 'Did he write anything about how he learned how to draw?'

'He wrote an essay called *But is it Art*?' the instructor said. 'In it he said, I wanted to learn to draw to convey an emotion I have about the beauty of the world. It's an appreciation of the mathematical beauty of nature, of how she works, a realisation that the phenomena we see result from the complexity of the inner workings of atoms.'

'Wow,' I said, 'that's inspirational. I never thought of drawing as a type of symbol.'

'He also said,' the instructor added. 'I've gotten so I like to draw nudes best. Even if it's not exactly art. That's why I thought you might also like drawing naked women .'

'Why? 'I asked.

'Because you're as weird as Feynman in your own way.'

'Thanks for the compliment.' I said. 'When do I get my Nobel prize?'

'There isn't one for drawing,' He said, 'but Auguste Rodin, the famous sculptor said. Man's naked form belongs to no particular moment in history; it is eternal, and can be looked upon with joy by the people of all ages. The body always expresses the spirit whose envelope it is. And for those who can see, the nude offers the richest meaning.'

If life drawing was a good enough hobby for Richard Feynman then it was good enough for me, There and then I decided that I would use the enforced 'freedom' of my retirement to learn about the aspects of humanity that could not be captured by my equations. I decided to ignore the easy attraction of the sweet strawberry t.v. couch and chase the swopping and swerving naked damsel flies of self-improvement out over the surging foam of the River Styx

This is the tale of my quest to learn how to draw, the thoughts and memories the experiences provoked, and the adventures I had in trying to develop my understanding of a new way of thinking. It is also tells how I came to terms with the fact that my public persona, developed over years of lecturing and teaching, was a mask for my true nature and that to really know myself I would have to remove that mask, reveal my soul and confront my humanity.

Chapter 1 The Basics of The Discipline.

It matters not what kind of figure-pictures you wish to paint, you will never be able to draw the figure properly, whether draped or otherwise, unless you have gone through a preliminary course of study from the nude.
– John Collier

'I suggest you start by enrolling for a life drawing class and learn how to become an artist,' the instructor said when I phoned him for more detailed advice. 'Until you have experienced the true artistic purpose of nudity you are going to confuse it with sexual flirtation or voyeurism. Life drawing can be a wonderful hobby to occupy your mind in retirement.'

'Do you mean while I wait to die?' I said.

He ignored me and continued. He was obviously an "Art Fanatic" and wasn't going to stop until I had heard him out.

In our society seeing people clothed is more natural than seeing them naked. Yet in the context of art, nudity is normal. Artists learn to view nude bodies as line, shape, value, form, volume, but when they draw from a living model they observe flesh, sensuality and sexuality. To prevent this becoming a sexual flirtation the artist stays hidden behind their clothes whilst the model is denied all cover. It is an unequal process but there is a sharing of basic truth about the human condition in the contact which you, Maurice my friend, immersed as you have been in your equations, have yet to experience.

As an artist you will learn that not all models are the same. Some know how to strike poses which are attractive, fluid and make life drawing a joy.

1

'How does a silent, unmoving model share thoughts and ideas?' I asked.

The instructor thought for a moment before continuing.

The artist can see the model's gestures, bodily and facial expressions, but also experiences a sharing of the model's inner self via the subtle body language of the human form. Body language is at its most powerful when the whole body takes part.

The human body has so many angles and curves and it's loaded with expectations and meaning. We know our bodies intuitively but not consciously. We can spot our species from afar, and pick out one friend among thousands. You must have scanned a crowd and been able to find a familiar face, even though all you had to go on were tiny differences, the cant of a nose, the minuscule differences in eye size or the relationship between ear and cheekbones.

We humans are not a telepathic species and yet we can communicate ideas and feeling without verbalizing them. We are used to reading subtle facial expression, and respond to the body movements of clothed individuals, but a nude model offers a much fuller range of body language to study.

Being able to find your mother in a herd is a lifesaving skill in evolutionary terms. Yet although we can spot Mom we often can't use words to describe her accurately to a police officer with an Indentikit. Without training in drawing we are quite unable to recall or sketch those features which we so easily recognize. That is the skill you learn from drawing.

In evolutionary terms, humans developed observational skills long before we invented clothes. As a species we have been walking on our hind legs for about three and a half million years, ever since an early ape called Lucy perfected the skill on the plains of Africa. We know from the fossil record we started walking upright about three and half million years ago. But it is the DNA of lice which tells the story of clothing. Lice can only survive on particular hosts or even on particular parts of particular hosts. Humans harbour three distinct types of lice. One lives in our pubic hair, another in our head hair and a third can only live In our clothing.

'I'm a mathematician not a biologist.' I said. 'What has this got to do with life drawing?'

'If you let me finish you'll find out.' The instructor said before continuing with his spiel.

The DNA of human pubic lice is closely related to that of the lice that live in gorilla's fur although we can't catch lice from a gorilla and they can't catch lice from us. The DNA sequencing of these lice cousins diverged three million years ago. That is when we lost our fur and grew a sparser covering of pubic hair instead. It didn't hide the detail of our body in the way fur did, so from then on we couldn't help but offer a sexual display to everyone we approached.

The DNA of our head and clothing lice are also related, but clothing lice can only live in human clothing and head lice (nits) in human hair. DNA sequencing shows this split happened about 70,000 years ago. That means we spent 293,000 years wandering around naked and furless while we got to know each other and formed tribes. We have worn clothes for just over 2% of the time we have existed as a species. Looked at in that evolutionary light, clothes are a recent innovation.

The implication of these facts is that our species' basic skills of recognition were honed by looking at naked bodies. This means life drawing is a return to an hereditary truth. When we discard all the visual baggage about rank, status and sexuality which clothing carries we tap into our neglected empirical heritage to see each other clearly and without

3

judgment. Artists break down their observations into components, lines, shadows, angles and curves. And yet the small inaccuracies we could accept when drawing an apple, a car or a building are magnified to unacceptability when drawing the body of a fellow human.

Our sense of bodily nuances is so highly tuned that the tiniest mis-observation in the angle of a nose ruins the likeness. Artists strive for accuracy, but if they draw too slowly, become too accurate or too calculated, they fail to capture the model's balance and weight. The drawing becomes a two dimensional cut-out instead of a body with mass and volume, it has no sense of the bone, muscle, and fat beneath the skin. It fails to capture the humanity, the personality, the character of the freely displayed soul. That drawing does not represent a breathing person but is a slab of flesh, an animal, a cadaver. The living spirit which they are striving to portray is not recorded in the marks on the paper.

Art teacher Betty Edwards says that the object of drawing is not only to show what you are trying to represent but also to show yourself. The more clearly you can perceive and draw what you see in the external world, the more clearly the viewer of your drawings can see you and the more you learn about yourself.

Seeing humans as they really are, is difficult, because it requires more than the cool, calm, objective sight that we use to draw still-life or landscape. We must learn to see the model's soul through the exposed flesh. We must suffuse our vision with feelings and respond to the living person. Human feeling is at the core of all successful art. Drawing the human body provides a chance to love yourself, and to relax without the need to wear a mask.

'But?' I interrupted as he finally paused for breath. 'How can I relax if I am clothed and am looking in judgment on the naked body of another person? Wearing good clothes is a symbol of status or honour, so wearing no clothes must be a symbol of poverty and shame.'

'When you stare at a naked human', the instructor said, 'there are no barriers, and you are reminded that you have more in common with the person you encounter than you might think. A nude individual reveals their essence, their soul, their self. How can it fail to relax you?'

When people take off their clothes, he went on as he got his second wind, they revert to their animal roots, and strip away their position in society. A real individual emerges from the camouflage of their chosen uniform.

When a model holds a long pose they have no chance to obscure the truth about their feelings. The artist can stare at every involuntary twitch. And once undressed and committed to the stillness of the pose, there's nowhere for the model to hide.

Early in her career in the 1930s, the American painter Alice Neel decided that she could only get to the soul of her subjects by painting them without clothes. Her last self-portrait, done at the age of eighty, shows her uncompromisingly nude. She believed the relationship between an artist and a model is a dialogue, and drawing a nude person requires a different kind of focus than depicting a still life. She said that drawing another human being is such a joyous opportunity, that both the artist and the model are changed for the better by it.

'Maurice,' the instructor said having finally completed his rant. 'I encourage you to enrol in a life drawing class and experience the creative contract of nudity between the artist and the model.'

5

'But I can't draw.' I protested.

'Get a book on it.' The instructor said, 'You keep telling your students the only real skill they learn from you is how to learn. Physician heal thy self.'

He was right, I knew that I needed to research the matter before I committed myself to such an alien discipline. Technical drawing is easy. I can simply produce an isometric projection if I have to. But drawing the untidy shapes of sagging human flesh is quite another matter. I learnt to draw with a tee-square, a pair of set-squares, a ruler and a pair of compasses. I still have the set of engineering drawing instruments I purchased as a student studying GCE 'O' Level Engineering Drawing, where I got a grade 1, which in those days was the top grade. But they will not help me draw humans who are not regular or linear in their lines and intercepts.

Before I could be confident enough to attend a drawing class I needed to discover more about the process of drawing. So I went along to the university library and asked the librarian if there was a good textbook on drawing people.

'You've been on the pre-retirement course, haven't you?' she said.

'How did you know?'

'I've had a run of elderly academics all looking for textbooks on how to do odd-ball things.' She said.

'Well do you have a book on drawing people?'

'Of course,' she said. 'You need Betty Edwards book, *Drawing on the Right Side of the Brain* and gave me the Dewy number.'

'That name rings a bell,' I said, 'The instructor quoted her.'

'That's because she's the best teacher of art ever.' The librarian said.

I was convinced, I picked up the book from its shelf, signed it out and took it home. I was surprised at how logical it was. I could quickly see that Prof Edwards was a teacher after my own heart. She had broken the technique of drawing down to into five basic skills which are.

1. Learning to see and copy edges.
2. Learning to see and draw empty space.
3. Learning to see and draw different objects in the correct relationship to each other.
4. Learning to see and draw light and shadow.
5. Learning to see and draw the whole of the composition and fit it on the page.

She had included exercises to help me develop each of these skills that I duly followed. She promised that once I had mastered these basics I would be able to develop further drawing skills which she described as drawing from memory and drawing from imagination. I decided not to worry about such lofty ambitions until I could manage to transcribe onto paper what I could see in front of me. If I was going to enrol in a drawing class I would have to be able to at least attempt to draw the model, or they would think I was just there to ogle naked flesh.

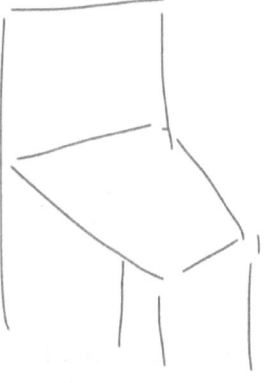

Dr Edward's basic idea was that as children we develop sets of symbols which we use to represent the things we see. But the symbols we use are not what we actually see. For example if I see a chair, I know the name for it and I have a readymade symbol for 'chair' which I draw instead of what I really see in front of me. My first exercise was to draw a chair. When I looked at it I knew Betty Edwards was right, it was simply a bad oblique projection of what I thought a chair was like.

The next task was to draw a strange collection of lines without trying to work out what the lines showed.

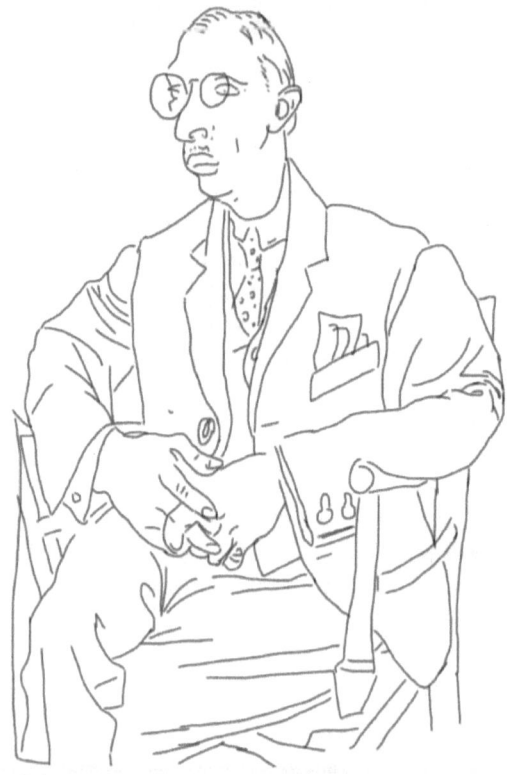

I did it, turned it over and found I had done a passable copy of Picassos' Portrait of Igor Stravinsky. That convinced me I might learn how to draw.

I eagerly started the next task which was to draw my own foreshortened hand using a sighting frame and a plastic sheet to draw the main shape, next I filled in the outline by drawing all the little lines and wrinkles.

It looked quite like my hand.

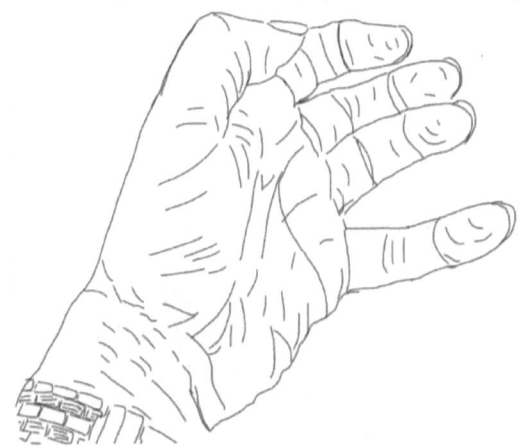

Now I had grasped the idea of drawing lines, and edges to make a reasonably recognisable drawing.

The next task was to draw a chair. But not the way I had tried at first. I had to look at where the chair, wasn't. i.e. at the empty space surrounding it then draw round the space that the chair occupied.

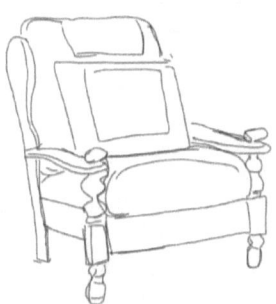

I tried this with a convenient arm-chair and found it worked.

This drawing of a chair was a great improvement on my first attempt.

I was beginning to get the idea of how to look and how to transcribe what I saw on the paper in front of me,

My next task was to draw a perspective drawing. I sat down and drew the corner of the emeritus

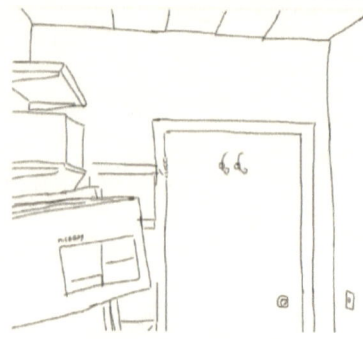

office I was in the process of moving into. The boxes of books still to unpack made a nice clutter on the left hand side.

Next I had to draw a face from the side.

I used my secretary as she didn't dare refuse.

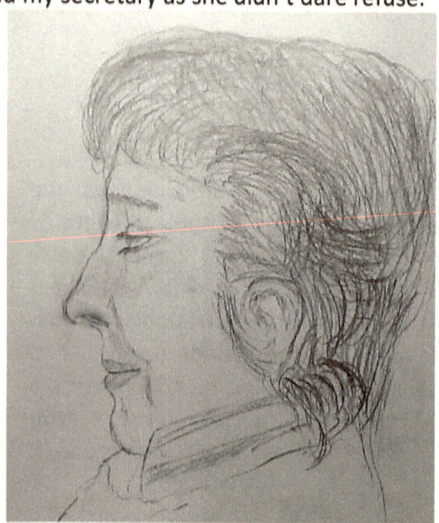

I don't think she enjoyed the experience but she was surprised that she could almost recognise herself from the sketch. I was even more surprised.

The next task in my work book was to study lights and shadows. There was a drawing by Gustave Courbet in the book, to draw upside down, but I had borrowed a book of drawings by Richard Feynman from the library, so I copied one of his nudes, upside down.

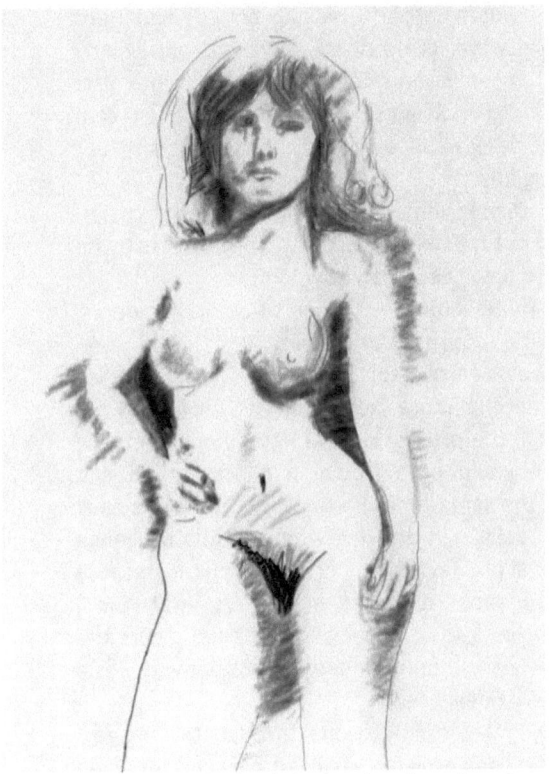

It has a few more lines that the Courbet drawing but is certainly made the point about shadows.

Richard Feynman, had started figure drawing in 1962, three years before he won his Nobel Prize in Physics. He had continued to draw, as a relaxing hobby over twenty five years, until his death in 1988. In 1995, Routledge, the academic publisher, published an illustrated book of his drawings. It is long out of print and costs a fortune to buy second hand, but I managed to borrow a copy through the university library. It's called *The Art of Richard P Feynman. Images by a Curious Character.*

The book opens with Feynman explaining how he first got interested in drawing. He wrote.

'Once I was at a party playing bongos and I got going pretty well. One of the guys was particularly inspired by my drumming. He went into the bathroom, took off he shirt, smeared shaving cream in funny designs all over his chest and came out dancing wildly.'

Clearly Dick Feynman went to some good parties. It turned out the dancing eccentric was an artist who offered to teach Feynman how to draw

Albert Hibbs, one of Feynman's doctoral students, said of Dick's approach to drawing.

'Dick was a puzzle solver, and the more complex the puzzle the more delightful the challenge! He took joy in the process. I have never known anyone else who could both frown in concentration and smile at the same time. Perhaps this is why he took so much delight in drawing women – the challenge of a special puzzle. I know part of the puzzle because he talked about it: What makes art, Art? And I believe he was especially puzzled by the attractiveness he found in a woman's body. It was a challenge he delighted in.'

This delight certainly shone through the image I had copied. His drawing revealed his soul, reflected from the soul of his model so the drawing is intensely personal yet still universal. I greatly enjoyed trying to copy it and felt I was sharing in Dick Feynman's thought processes as I tried to emulate the spontaneous lines he had used to capture the essence of his model.

His daughter Michelle, who edited the book of his drawings said about him.

'I assumed all scientists had some creative outlet... but not all scientists shared such a passion for drawing. It seemed perfectly natural that every Monday evening after supper, a lithesome young woman would knock at the door and come into our home, soon to descend with Papa into his study downstairs for several hours. I used to go down to Papa's study and peek at his drawings. To be honest the nudity did not shock me, but I did find it funny - I could easily see when a body was out of proportion so the model looked too fat or too thin. I remember being surprised when I discovered a drawing of a model with her clothes on, and wondered, what was wrong with her?'

I was beginning to feel that there was a something to interest me in learning to draw. Feynman has long been one of my mathematical heroes and now he was turning into a role model for how to enjoy drawing.

The next task was to draw a three quarter view of a face showing not just the lines but the shadows too. I didn't have a willing model and felt I daren't press my secretary into service again as she might feel I was harassing her. I asked my family but they all refused, then one afternoon whilst sitting in the garden of our holiday cottage sketching the house, my nephew fell asleep on a reclining deck chair. I took the opportunity to draw him, with shadows as well as lines.

When he woke up I showed him the sketch and thanked him for modelling.

'It's ok,' he said, 'But I'm glad you told me it was me,' which I took as a rather backhanded compliment.

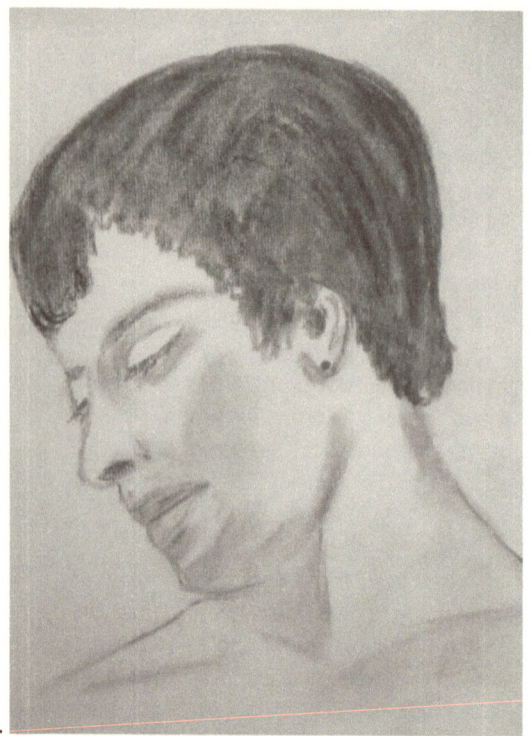

By now I was beginning to feel that I might be able to learn how to draw so I plucked up my courage and enrolled on a life drawing course.

Chapter 2 The Naked and the Nude

Absolute nakedness is intrusive, confusing to the senses.
Paradoxically, it both reveals and diminishes identity
- P D James

Now I had mastered the rudiments of drawing I was ready to attend the life drawing class at the local Evening Institute. I bought various sizes of sketch pads, a selection of pencils and a new rubber.

Completely equipped, I presented myself on the appointed evening and was surprised to find that the instructor was a charming young lady who I shall call Deborah. She was enthusiastic, had bright pink hair, wore dungarees and was delightfully wacky as she introduced herself to the class. She told us she was a professional artist who taught life drawing part time in order earn enough to eat, but that she enjoyed taking the class because by trying to pass on her visual skills she learned so much about her own short-comings.

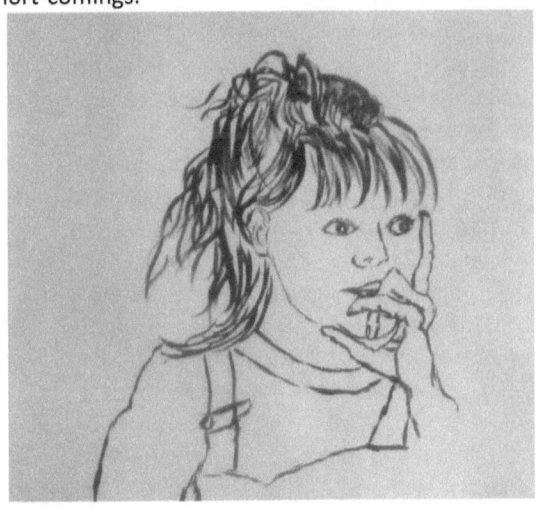

Having spent a professional lifetime lecturing and tutoring I could identify with this, as I also had learned as a young lecturer that the best way to learn something is to teach it.

My fellow students were a mixed bunch. There were some young artists, who said they wanted the practice and some old codgers, like me, who needed something to do. But we all shared an interest in learning how to draw. Among the more mature students I spotted another refugee from the pre-retirement course, Professor Austin Sheerline, I nodded to him, and to a lady whom I knew as a primary school teacher, who had taught my children. I shall call her Alice.

'I didn't expect to meet you here.' I said to Alice. 'Surely drawing naked people is a bit racy for a retired teacher?'

'It's artistic and cultural and it's also very satisfying.' she said, grinning at me. 'I didn't know you could draw.'

'I can't,' I replied, 'That's why I've come to learn.'

At this point in the proceedings a large lady wearing a pink bath robe entered the studio and stood on the small raised stage-like area, which Deborah referred to as 'the stand'. Deborah went over to speak to her and then spoke to the class. She looked like a mouse squaring up to an elephant. The large model smiled at her, and the smile lit up her face. She looked a jolly roly-poly. I immediately felt that if I had met her at a dinner party I would have enjoyed her company.

'We'll start with some quick gesture poses.' Deborah said. 'Just take your sketch book and pencil and try and capture the main lines of each pose.' She looked at the model. 'Are you ready Eileen?' she said.

The model nodded and took off her bath robe. She was even larger without it than she had been wearing it. She was about five foot five tall and I estimated that she must have weighed about 25 stone. She was big and buxom. She held her arms up and stood quite still.

Wow, I thought. She's got guts to do that!

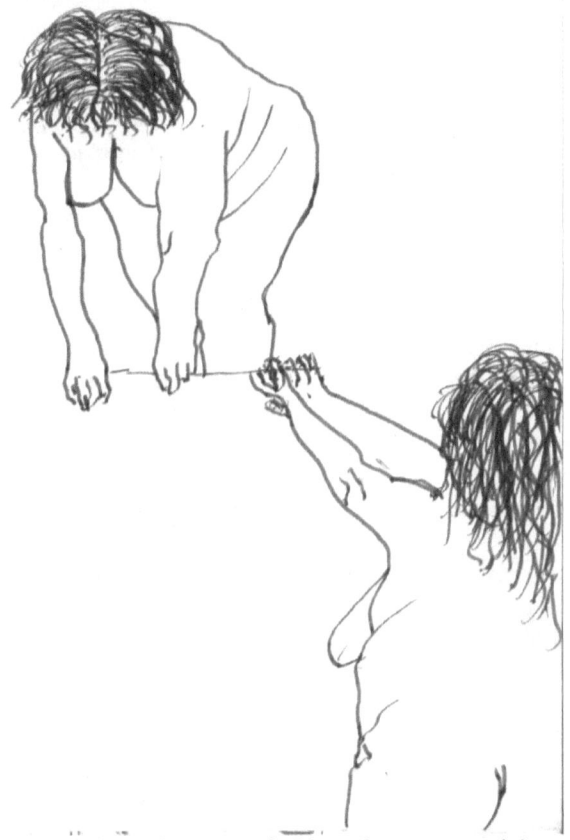

Alice whispered to me. 'I like Eileen to model there's so much of her to draw.'

I just smiled, I was too awe-struck to speak. Rubinesque didn't do her justice and she was so confident.

'Off you go,' Deborah said. 'Just try and draw what you see in front of you.'

That was when I first realized that creating an image of the human form from a living breathing model is a good way to develop both the mechanical skill of making marks on a piece of paper and the spiritual skill of observing and understanding human nature. I could see how drawing from a living model would develop my artist's eye. The fact a model can only hold a pose for a limited time forced choices on me. I had to capture what I saw while it remained in place. Even slight changes in posture completely changed the pose.

This rapid, time-limited, process demanded my total concentration. Nothing apart from the shape and detail of the model, and the marks needed to reproduce this inner perception, could happen in my mind. Such complete absorption made time cease and only the model's physical need to move, and relieve cramping muscles, interrupted my process of observation and rendition.

Eileen's naked presence was an elemental force of nature. Clothed I saw her as a fat, dowdy, middle-aged women. Nude she was the original Earth Mother of pagan myth.

I quickly became absorbed in drawing and stopped thinking in words as the detail of drawing became intensely interesting. Things were going well and I felt 'locked onto' the personae I was trying to render into crafted line. This state of enhanced perception was extremely pleasant and when I finished drawing I found I wasn't tired from the concentration but refreshed by the insight I had gained into aspects of Eileen I would never have noticed if I simply passed her in the street.

During the evening she did two much longer seated poses but the power of her presence was not diminished by sitting down. An elemental authority arose from her naked body and commanded respect.

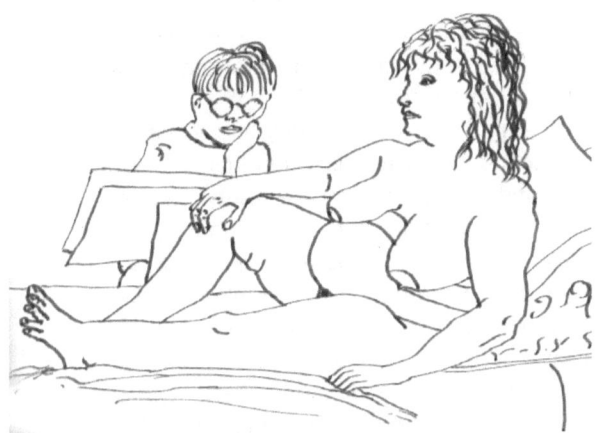

When the session finished, Deborah called a halt to the class. Eileen put on her pink robe and left the room. She had not once spoken to us. As we students were packing up she emerged from the side room transformed into a middle-aged overweight woman in a long skirt, woolly coat and hat, carrying a Tesco bag which contained her pink bathrobe and slippers.

'Bye, everyone,' she said and smiled that wonderful, warming smile. I found it hard to relate this mediocre shabby housewife, rushing off to catch her bus home, with the living exciting Willendorf Venus whose breasts and loins I, along with my fellow students, had been struggling to confine to the limits of our sketch pads.

I had a joyful and enlightening introduction to life drawing. Nothing apart from the shape and detail of the model, and the marks needed to reproduce my inner perception, mattered while I was drawing. Absorbed in drawing, I felt 'locked into' the person I was rendering as a crafted line.

The human animal is the only creature which has an ability, and even a need, to filter the world through its senses, intellect and soul, and then spit it out as a drawing. Now I recognised that we get our highest levels of satisfaction from drawing fellow humans. But what drives this need?

Is life drawing simply about nudity and sexuality? Certainly a nude model wilfully puts their sexuality on display. And raw naked human sexuality has been a legitimate part of art from its very beginning, tens of thousands of years. The cave paintings of Lascaux and Altamira, and the contemporary plump naked Venus figurines, demonstrate this. I cannot deny that I share our species continuing interest in sexuality and when I draw from a nude model there must be some latent sexual dimension to the interaction.

To stand close to the naked body of a stranger and examine it closely, is an unusual experience in modern society. During the life drawing session I shared an intimate view of the model, yet I was held at a prudent distance.

The tradition of life drawing is a sort of theatre performance which centres on an unclothed person in a room with an audience of clothed perceivers who are expected to observe the naked model scientifically and objectively, without eroticism or judgmental feelings. Life drawing is built on this myth of impartial observation. But why do clothed humans want to draw naked humans in these strange circumstances? It was as much a puzzle for me as it had been for Dick Feynman. Perhaps an answer lay in thinking about the function of clothing.

Clothing individualizes a person and slots them into an economic context, or a particular time and place. But human virtues and vices are timeless. If we take away a model's clothing we remove all the external references that clothes give rise to. A naked body raises no questions of political motive, class, economic or social status. Nakedness is universal and eternal, it is the bedrock of human nature. The undraped figure is the most physically, psychologically complex and powerful form we can ever attempt to reduce to two-dimensional marks on paper.

To deter any erotic overtones and maintain control and propriety in this unusual situation, two different concepts 'nude' and 'naked' have been defined.

In the context of Art a model is 'nude'. This involves a complex set of agreements between the model, the artist and society. You can be naked anywhere, all you need to do is take off your clothes. But you can only be nude when someone is looking at you. Nakedness on its own is straightforward, it's the context, the audience and the agreement to be observed that is involved in nudity which makes it different from simply being unclothed.

A model allows an artist to stare at each and every part of their body without any attempt to conceal those parts which are normally only displayed to intimate friends in a sexual context. A model may agree to pose in ways which would be considered lewd if done it public. It is the model's choice to be without clothes. A model is nude and a nude is an object of artistic veneration, unlike a naked person who is someone deprived of clothes and consequently stripped of the protection and badges of rank which their clothes confer. Nakedness can be accidental, or voluntary but it lacks mutual agreement to be stared at by an observer. If the lack of clothes is accidental the naked person is embarrassed when observed by a clothed intruder. If the lack of clothes is intentional, say as part of a domestic practice, such as undressing to go to bed, and is done in front of a regular partner there is no embarrassment or any particular intent. But if the nakedness is a form of sexual exhibitionism which the individual intends to culminate in a carnal outcome, a view which may or may not be shared by the observer, it can be intrusive and lewd.

Formal nudity licenced me to view, examine and record any details of the model's body which seemed interesting, without inhibition, without any implied invitation to sexual intimacy or any guilt about voyeuristic intrusion. Detailed observation of a nude is intended to exclude guilt, intrusiveness or sexual invitation. But it also means that if you choose to attend life drawing class you give up any right to prudery. You have agreed not to be offended or annoyed by the exposure of private parts.

Society imposes public rules of dress and conventions on body exposure, but it encourages blatant displays of the unclothed nude human body in artistic situations. Yet to a person walking unaware into the drawing studio the model is 'naked'. The difference between nude and naked is a matter of perception and agreement.

Kenneth Clark, writing in his book *The Nude: A Study in Ideal Form* said:

To be naked is to be deprived of our clothes, and the word implies the embarrassment most of us feel in that condition. The word 'nude,' on the other hand, carries, in educated usage, no uncomfortable overtone. The image it projects into the mind is not of a huddled and defenceless body, but of a balanced, prosperous, and confident body: the body re-formed.

Viewing a naked body sums up everything we aspire to, and everything we most fear. The human body is the source of our deepest pleasures and our most profound traumas. To be unclothed can mean humiliation, discomfort, or exposure, or it can mean satisfying our most profound narcissistic and intimate needs.

To see another person naked might reassure us or alarm us, it might satisfy our curiosity or provoke our guilt, it might arouse our desire or our disgust. The exposed adult body preserves memories of a lost wholesomeness of infancy whilst pre-empting faint corrupt seeds of future dissolution and death. We bring nothing into this life and we can take nothing from it. We are born naked and we rot naked in death. The mystique of the nude is a powerful combination of exposure and control. The model is revealed, by the absence of clothing yet the artist can control the model, through drawing, in order to express the deep truth represented by the exposed body.

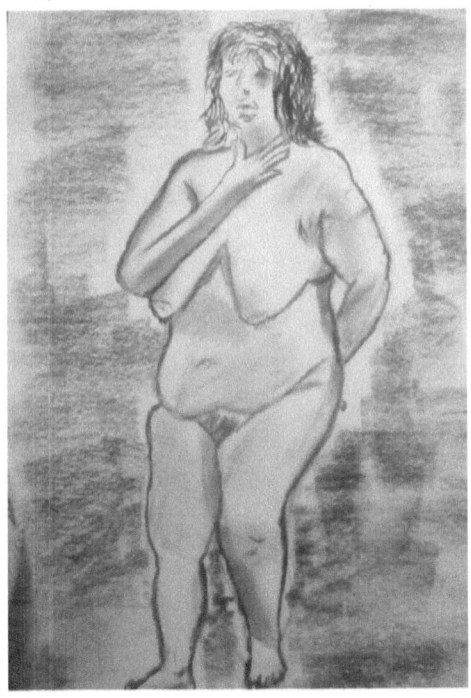

Chapter 3 Developing An Artist's Eye

Man's naked form... belongs to no particular moment in history; it is eternal, and can be looked upon with joy by the people of all ages.
—Auguste Rodin

I had been told that artists talk of nude bodies in terms of line, shape, value, form, volume, yet after my first class I knew they draw from a living model and observed skin, sensuality and sexuality.

My first life drawing session had made me deeply aware that the artist hides behind clothes whilst the model sheds all of theirs. It is a highly unequal state of affairs so what do artist and model gain from this practice? If they did not both get something from the experience they would not do it.

As I attended more classes I noticed that not all models are the same. Some know how to strike poses which are attractive, graceful and make drawing a pleasure.

A good model is incredibly interactive. Eileen, can keep still for long poses and is obliging, open and affable. But some models are not so good, they fidget and take up closed poses that reveal as little of themselves as possible.

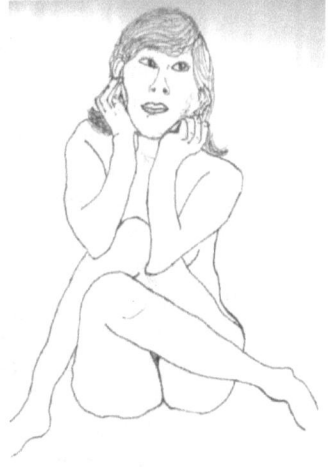

I see the model's gestures, bodily and facial expressions, but also experience a subtle sharing of the model's inner self via the mysterious body language of the naked human form. Humans are not telepathic but we can communicate ideas and feeling without verbalizing. We are used to reading subtle facial expression, and responding to the body language of clothed individuals, but when we draw a nude model a much fuller range of body language is on view.

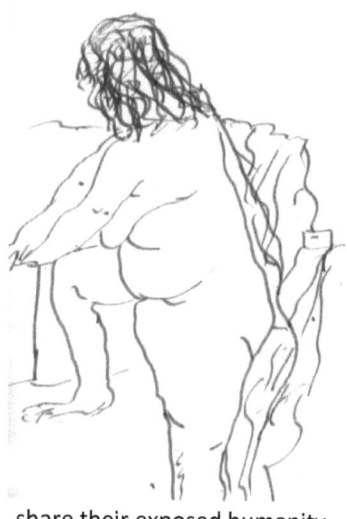

A good model manages to say many things without moving. By opening up their soul and caring about making Art, they inspire the artist with a welcome message to share their exposed humanity.

They produce a sensuality of observation, and an intimacy of drawing, which stimulates creativity in every sense. Yet even as they evoke purity, passion and humanity the model's nudity can still feel disquieting, transgressive and surprising. As I draw a nude I reach for a fundamental link with a pureness of being that grows out of a voluntary sharing of the deepest of human feelings. I feel privileged to enter a space which is normally intensely private.

The model contracts to unveil their nakedness to pose for me. This contract involves communion, compassion, mutual civility and payment, yet the model's voluntary nudity still moves me profoundly.

Our shared task, of creating a life drawing, demands that we both look beyond the strangeness and discomfort we might normally feel about nakedness and in staring and being stared at. Certainly the model is paid, but the fee is so small it merely shows the model is valued, rather than making them rich. The model must get more than the fee from the transaction and I was curious what else motivated them.

Salvidor Dali said that when drawing from a nude model, the artist should feel naked. I suspect by this he meant that an artist must identify with what they see. You must seek that inner soul that the nude model cannot avoid revealing during a long pose.

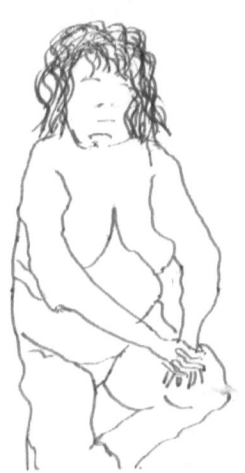

False smiles, false sincerity and false modesty cannot be sustained over a forty-five minute pose. It is an act of great generosity when a model conjures up a basic human feeling and illustrates it with their body language. When it happens I find I am pulled into the drawing. The intense concentration releases me from the distractions and hidden nuances of normal life and focuses my mind on line, form and shadow until I finish, stand back, and view the complete drawing. Only then do I understand the emotion and meaning I have been trying to capture.

Drawing a nude model is difficult. A body has many angles and curves to transcribe and it's loaded with expectations and meaning. We humans know our bodies intuitively but not consciously. We can spot our species from afar, and pick out our friend among thousands.

I had been told, that evolution developed these observational skills long before we invented clothes. Yet today we rarely see an unclothed stranger in the flesh. When we do, we have to ditch all our cultural baggage and try to tap into our neglected empirical heritage to see emotion and intent clearly and without pre-judgment. We break our observations down into components, lines, shadows, angles and curves. And yet the small inaccuracies are magnified unacceptably when drawing a naked human. Our sense of body nuances is so highly tuned that the tiniest mis-observation ruins a likeness. I strive for accuracy, but if I draw too slowly, become too accurate or too calculated, I fail to capture the model's essence. The laboured drawing becomes a two dimensional cut-out instead of a body with mass and volume, it has no sense of bone, muscle, and fat beneath the skin. I fail to capture the humanity, the personality, the

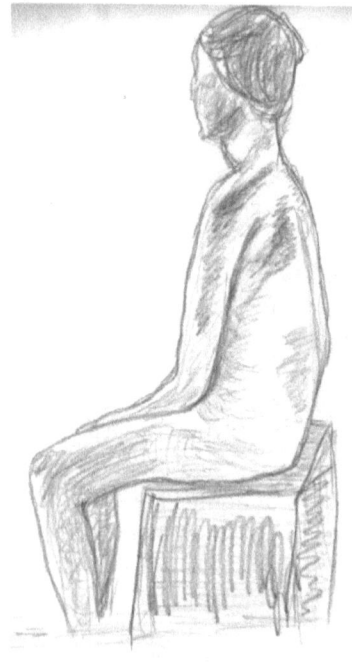

character, the freely displayed soul. It is a diagram of the flesh not a portrait of a living being.

Seeing humans as they really are, is difficult. It requires more than the cool, calm, objective sight that I use to draw still-life or landscape. I have to practice so that I learn to see the model's soul through its subtle influence on the exposed skin. Human empathy is at the core of all successful Art.

To draw a model and make the viewer feel they are looking at a real person, artists must transcend technique and show how they feel about that individual, about the world, and themselves. They must reveal their own soul, reflected by the soul of the model. When they succeed, the truth of the drawing becomes intensely personal yet completely universal.

Drawing a human body provides a chance to love yourself, and to relax without the need for masks. You meet another human without barriers. Life drawing challenges you to accept a person on all levels. That is why it evokes such a wonderful honesty.

I was beginning to feel a deep satisfaction in drawing from life. The satisfaction grew as my drawings took shape. The initial intense period of concentration banished all thoughts from my mind, accept those needed for drawing, and time stopped while I studied detail. As I become more aware of the model, and of my developing drawing skills, I become more conscious of myself. My study of the model's nude body, became an act of humility in which I forgot physical frailties and imperfections, and marvelled at the diversity of the human form stripped of the protection of clothing.

This line of thought made me think again about why we wear clothes. Your choice of clothing affects you mentally more than you realise. For example if you want to run a successful hardware store then you must wear a brown overall otherwise nobody will take you seriously. If you want to project the reassuring bedside manner of a doctor you need a white coat and stethoscope round your neck

Progressively, over the centuries, society has cultivated clothing as a mask. It was originally developed to protect people from the elements of heat and cold, to stop them from getting burned or frozen. Then it became a method of adornment to enhance attractiveness and a prop for ritual and ceremonial purposes. In latter centuries, we have formed an unhealthy cultural dependency on clothing. Now clothes are a mask to hide our personality and character deficiencies. They are a way of concealing the intentions which the body language of a naked human openly admits to. A nude person has to reveal their all.

To capture this essence on paper involves a co-ordination of hand and eye that perhaps only a surgeon or a chef would understand.

Life drawing challenges you to accept a person's form at all levels. It challenges you to reduce a complex three dimensional moving, breathing object to a two dimensional emotional symbol.

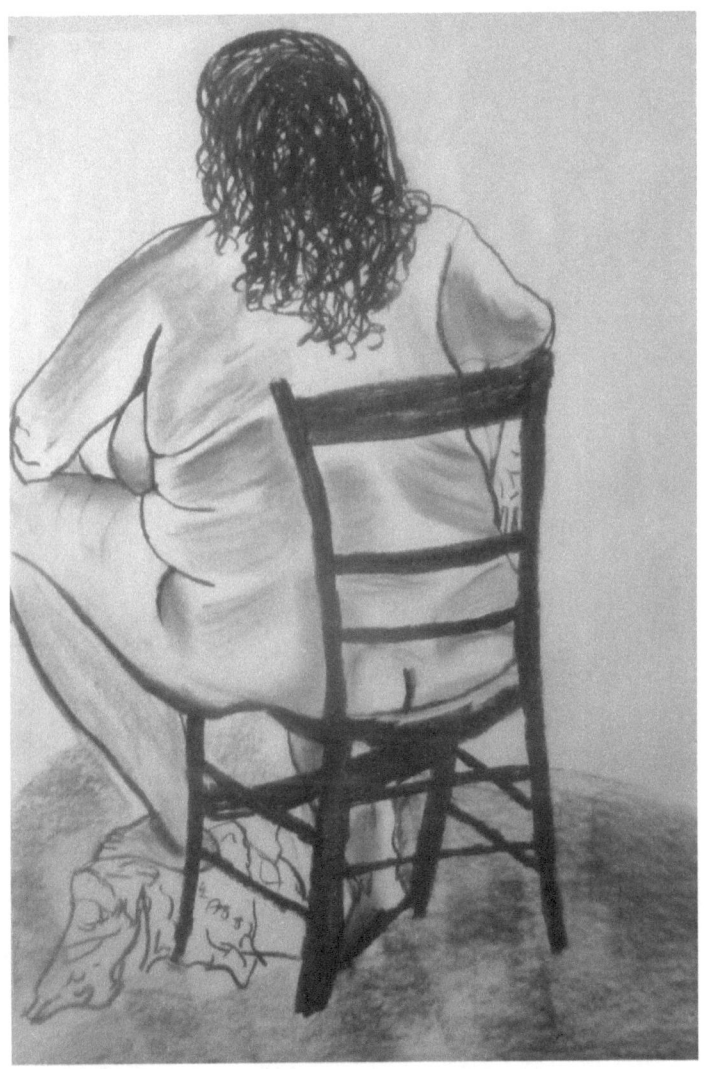

Chapter 4 The Armour of Clothing

Don't judge the people by their clothes.. however you might be able to judge them spontaneously when they are naked.'
—*Toba Beta*

When it was first suggested to me that I might enjoy drawing naked people I thought the idea sounded rather deviant, not erotically but exploitatively. The relationship between me, a fully clothed artist and a naked model, obliged to submit to my every visual whim, would be totally unequal. As an artist I could choose the pose, interpret the viewpoint, order the model to remove their clothes, instruct them how hold themselves, insist they do not fidget while I stare relentlessly at those parts of their body they would not normally reveal to strangers. I couldn't help but think that the model must feel vulnerable. Yet I had sensed a power in the happily revealed bare skin of Eileen in my first life drawing lessons.

Having lived for most of my professional life in the academic environment which created political correctness and enforced gender equity I felt uncomfortable with what appeared to be the artistic self-obsession and arrogance of forcing a fellow human to strip and abase themselves for my amusement. Let's face it the only reason I was taking up drawing was for my own pleasure, nobody was going to buy my scribblings, so I couldn't even offer the excuse that it was a necessary evil I must endure in order to make a living. Being retired I no longer needed to make a living. I was doing it for fun. But even with my monumental lack of skill, I would still be legally able to sign my daubings whilst my model would be condemned to remain forever an unidentified, anonymous chunk of meat, whose sole purpose was to reflect light from their private regions. Why would anybody offer to dispense with the protection of their clothing in the name of art?

We use clothing to project an image that is different from our self-perceived inner reality. By covering up our bodies we hide any personality or emotional defects we think we have. By concealing our bodies behind clothing we mask our reality, hide our weaknesses and emotionally protect ourselves.

Our clothes are not just a means of concealment, they offer protection akin to a suit of armour. Wearing clothes, can hide your identity and make you into someone much grander. Without them, everything hangs out for all to see, every emotional response, every erotic seepage is on show. A clothed male can conceal an erection, but a naked man is shamed by his evident arousal. A clothed woman can be coy, but a naked woman makes herself available to the prurient gaze of every male present.

We humans are the only species of ape to wear clothes. And it is relatively recent social innovation to believe it is important never to been seen without them. But why did our species of ape, start to wear clothes? I can think of only four reasons.

1. *For Protection*
2. *To Show Social Status*
3. *To maintain decency*
4. *For decoration and to make ourselves attractive*

Like most people I dress differently for social encounters than for formal events. Out of statistical curiosity I decided to work out what dress codes I have followed over the last 40 years and to what extent. The results surprised me. The way I dress depends a great deal on whom I expect to meet. When I know that I am going to be observed, and that I will be judged on what I am wearing, I conform to pre-set expectations. When I think I will not be seen I behave differently.

Whilst I still worked at the university my dress code was what I would describe as smart causal, i.e. jacket, trousers and open necked shirt, I would dress in a similar fashion when giving public lectures or meeting colleagues. If I went to my local Rotary Club I would wear a dark suit, white shirt and tie. If I was not working I would wear a sweater with either jeans or causal trousers, and if I was going outside I would put on an anorak. During the summer holidays I might wear shorts, with or without a shirt, depending on the temperature. When I attended graduation ceremonies I would always wear full academic dress over a formal suit and collage tie.

But what proportion of my 40 years as a professor, a mathematician and a university administrator, have I spent conforming to each of these five different styles of dress code?

I have spent just over five years wearing smart causal dress, six months wearing a formal business suit and about the same time wearing shorts. I have spent only a month wearing academic dress but about twenty-three years wearing sweaters and causal trousers. This adds up to about 24 years. What did I wear for the other sixteen years? It was only when I totalled up the time that I realized I had spent 16 of the last 40 years completely naked.

Let me explain how I arrived at this rather surprising figure for a respectable academic who is neither a nudist nor a naked protester.

Ever since I married I have slept without the encumbrance of clothing. As I enjoy sleeping I have spent on average at least seven and sometime ten hours a day in bed. This means that for 40% of my academic life I have not worn anything.

Few people will be aware that I spend 40% of my life naked, because I remove my clothing in the privacy of my own home. However during those sixteen naked years it is not surprising that a handful of friends have seen me *au naturel*. Those observers who have encountered me in my birthday suit have been house guests either at my main home or more likely at the various rural holiday cottages in remote corners of the Lake District, I have owned over the years.

Let me tell you a little about my first rural hovel and the simple life style it encouraged me to lead during holiday periods before my wife and I traded up to a bungalow with an indoor bathroom. It was a small cottage set in five acres of its own land, well away from the road and not overlooked. All of the friends who stayed with my wife and me there, had known us for years and many had gone to university with us, so we had shared communal changing rooms, played sports and been swimming with them.

The cottage had a separate outside toilet and one cold water tap. As we would stay down there for the whole summer the needs of cleanliness soon overcame false modesty. If the weather was warm neither we, nor our guests, wore much more than shorts and tee shirt about the house, or swimwear at the beach. If anyone wanted to wash at the end of the day then they would heat water in the kettle, fill a washing up bowl, take it outside where we kept an old washstand between the kitchen door and the outside loo. There in the field just behind the cottage, we simply stripped off and washed ourselves down before pouring the remains of the bowl over ourselves. Among my old photo albums I found some photos my wife had taken of our friend Tony at his evening abolitions and of me wandering back from the loo passing Sheila, Tony's wife as she is having a morning strip-wash. I have made sketches from the snaps.

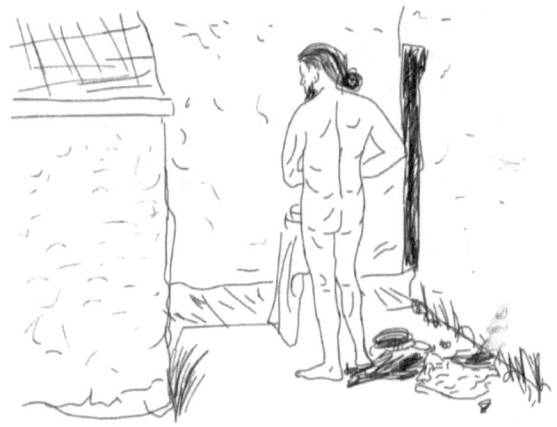

As you can see in those days we weren't shy.

The cottage's single room was partitioned off at one end to form an almost separate bedroom with a double bed, there was another double bed settee in the living room and an open attic with two small beds upstairs. We soon found that all our close friends were just as used to sleeping naked as we were. All things considered we were all products of the hedonistic sixties. As the loo was outside in a separate outhouse, if anyone needed to go they rarely bothered to dress unless it was particularly cold outside, which it rarely was in the summer. We spent a lot of time by the sea, and often had the beaches almost to ourselves. Most of our friends enjoyed

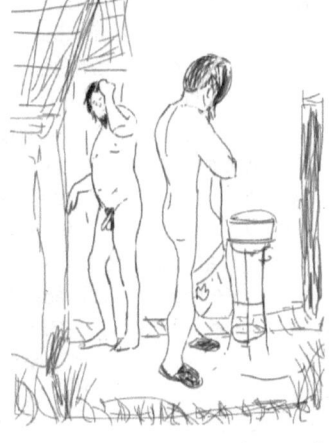

the freedom and bohemian student atmosphere of our summer breaks and never put much effort into trying to maintain any sort of clothed dignity. This carefree hedonism continued even after we all moved on to take up more senior academic careers.

We washed ourselves in the field behind the house and we washed our kids in a plastic baby bath in front of the living room fire. During those summer months that simple cottage was really just a big communal dormitory.

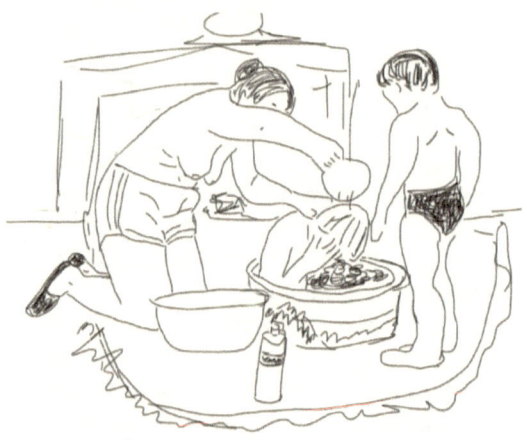

If we wanted to change into swimsuits at the beach we simply stripped off and changed. I am quite sure that many of my professional colleagues, and most of my fellow Rotarians, would be quite shocked at the casual attitude towards clothing that I shared with my close friends and family then.

This brings me back to my question of why do people feel they have to wear clothes all the time?

I am aware that clothes affect me mentally, perhaps even more than I like to admit. When I wear academic dress I feel important. When I wear smart causal I feel professional. When I wear a suit I feel respectable but at the end of the day when I retire to my bed and drop my clothes on the bedroom floor, I feel relaxed and natural. I discard my inhibitions and my worries with my body covering.

Before the seventeenth century almost everyone slept naked and only wore underclothes during the day to protect their main garments from interior staining. But in these days of central heating there does not seem to be any practical reason to wear clothing when sleeping indoors. Additional warmth and protection is provided by bedding. Yet despite the lack of any logical need for night wear recent surveys have found only about a quarter of the population sleep naked. Among unmarried people about 30% of men, and around 17% of women, wear nothing to bed. For married couples this changes to about one in five couples (20%) who sleep together nude.

I am not alone in spending more than a third of my life without bothering to dress but I am not in the majority. However, during my daily social and professional life I am far more conformist. I have to consider what others think about my clothes and I always wear clothing once I have left my bed, except for the occasional walk to the shower in a morning. But once showered I dress, according to the dress code which applies to what I intend to do, I remained dressed until bedtime.

I soon discovered that the life room has its own rules and the artist must wear the uniform of his/her artistic rank whilst the model is always naked. It is a contract both parties agree to. The model must wear a uniform of nudity when in pose and put on a robe at all other times. To be without clothes whilst not in pose is considered embarrassing to both model and artist.

Progressively, over the centuries, society has developed clothing as a complex mask, capable of carrying subtle messages to groups of observers. It may originally just have been used to protect people from the elements of heat and cold, to stop them from getting sunburn or frostbite. But it has now become a method of adornment to enhance attractiveness or a prop for ritual and ceremonial purposes. Today we have a lifestyle dependency on clothing and a cultural fear of nakedness. We use clothes to hide our personality and character deficiencies. We fear the detailed body language that a naked human cannot avoid projecting may influence observers to react unfavourably towards us and so we don't intentionally let anyone but our sexual partners, see us naked.

I know I use clothing to project an image that is different from my self-perceived inner reality. I use clothing to deny others sight of my true self. I clothe myself to disguise my animal urges, hide my emotions and protect myself from the invasive judgement of society's observers. But, as Mark Twain pointed out, nobody listens to a naked man. Once you take off your clothes you forfeit the respect of society. But the degree of reversion seems to depend entirely on the exact circumstances of the exposure and the mutually agreed attitudes of the naked person being observed and the state of dress of the observer.

I can perhaps best illustrate this by telling a little anecdote about myself, a trival incident which took place early one morning at my current holiday home. It is a modern bungalow with indoor plumbing in deference to my lofty professorial status, rather than the simple rustic hovel I owned as a young academic.

It was daylight when I was woken by my wife getting quietly out of bed, slipping on a nightdress and going to the loo. As she went into the corridor I looked at the bedside clock and saw it was 7:15. She came back, removed her nightdress and lay down beside me. I tried to doze off again but I couldn't settle back to sleep. The evening before, when we and the visitors who were staying with us, had returned from a meal out, I had drunk half a bottle of white wine, just before going to bed. Although I had enjoyed it at the time now I could feel the pressure of my alcoholic indulgence in my bladder. I looked at the clock and saw it was 7:40. The house was quiet, My wife had gone back to sleep. She had covered her nakedness because we had house-guests but I thought she was being over fussy. If we had been alone in the house she would not have bothered to wear anything just to visit the loo. Nobody was likely to get up for at least another hour, so why bother with clothes? By now I had a pressing need to go but I didn't have any compelling need to put on clothing as I was not going to be observed.

I slipped out of bed and made my way quietly along the corridor to the bathroom and relieved myself as silently as I could, so as not to wake our guests. I flushed the toilet and began to make my way back to bed. As I was about to step through the bathroom door into the corridor I heard the guest bedroom door open and footsteps sound on the corridor. One of our guests was on their way to the loo. This was not part of my plan. I had not expected to be observed naked but I was about to be.

To get back to my bedroom I had to walk along the corridor towards the guest bedroom. Our house guests were a highly respectable retired clergyman, a Revd. expert in theology and his wife. And I had already started to step out through the bathroom door so my foot and lower leg was already visible to whoever was out there, even though I could not yet see who it was. It was too late to close the bathroom door. I was partway through the doorway and balanced on one leg.

A range of lurid scenarios flashed through my mind. What if our guests slept *sans* clothes, as many of my old collage friends did. What if the visiting wife had decided to slip to the loo in the early morning expecting no one else to be up and about. What if I was about to meet her and to have to brush passed her in that narrow corridor, with both of us in a state of undress?

There was no way I could cover myself without drawing excessive attention to my nakedness. Trying to hide my genitals with my hands would only look like I was playing with myself and would make my brazen display much worse than simply acting as though I was dressed. A naked encounter would have been fine with any of my old college friends. We had all shared outdoor sponge baths, nude sun bathing on remote beaches and skinny dipping escapades in our misspent youth. We would simply have said 'Good Morning' and squeezed passed. But I did not know our present guests that well, they were professional academic acquaintances, not long term intimates sharing a mutually hedonistic hippy heritage from the nineteen sixties.

Was I about to stand naked in front of a properly dressed respectable lady, or potentially more embarrassing, before a properly undressed respectable lady? I was not worried about the legality of exposing myself, as I was in my own house so my nakedness was both legal and natural. But I was concerned about intruding on the privacy of a lady who was not expecting to meet her host *au naturel* and might not be dressed in a manner such that she would welcome scrutiny.

Time seemed to almost stop in those brief microseconds as I stepped out into the corridor. I mentally prepared myself to meet a naked, or at best scantily clad, female social acquaintance on the corridor. I knew that at all costs I must avoid embarrassing her as I inflicted my nudity on her.

There was an imbalance of power, and of foreknowledge, in the impending encounter. I knew I was naked and as I had to complete the step out into the corridor I was committed to revealing my all to whoever was now moving along the corridor towards the bathroom door. I did not know if it would be my Revd friend or his wife, and I did not know if the individual was dressed or undressed.

I quickly reviewed my options. My major concern was how to conduct my uncovered form in front of a respectable lady guest who might be as naked as I was. Would I be able to avoid looking down at her body if she too was sky clad? Women always know if a man is looking at their body, no matter how surreptitious he tries to hide his gaze. I have on occasions met old female college friends in similar early morning excursions, both naturally dressed in our birthday suits, and I have never been able to avoid looking down at their bodies. But they have never pretended not to look at me either. We both know we are no sexual threat to each other so any staring is just friendly curiosity. But my lady guest had no such past experiences with me and I had no idea how she might respond if she felt I was ogling her exposed and sexually vulnerable body. Would she scream and waken the whole household?

I had no option but to complete that step out into the corridor that I had started to take before I heard the bedroom door open. If I tried to pull back I would lose my balance and fall down in an even more revealing heap on the floor in front of her or, perhaps worse, blunder into her whilst trying to remain upright. If that happened I would not be able to pretend I was not looking at her. Avoiding a charge of opportunist voyeurism or even inappropriate touching in such circumstances would be difficult. Embarrassing scenarios of being unable to conceal bodily indications of sexual arousal also raised worrying possibilities in my mind. My guest was approaching an intimate social encounter quite unaware of what was about to happen.

My heart began to pound as I realised what a dilemma I had created by ignoring the dress code of normal community intercourse. But my die was cast, my body bare, my genitals on show and I was balanced on the boundary of total exposure. There was nothing else I to do but step out into the corridor and face the consequences of my earlier choice.

Reflecting with hindsight, I wonder why I felt so embarrassed about what should have been a simple situation? It would not be the first time I had been naked in the presence of a friend's unclothed wife.

I was not panicking about innocently exposing myself in my own house. But I was deeply concerned about the possibility of intruding on the privacy of a lady who was not expecting to have to visually engage with my sexual organs. How could I avoid embarrassing her?

I recall thinking what Jung had said about Japanese naked mixed bathing customs in the *konyoko* style hot tubs. He had written about avoiding 'the indiscreet glance' when the social niceties demand that one be completely naked but expected to guard against overtly staring at the sexual organs of fellow bathers of either sex. This memory offered me a way forward. I could wish the lady good morning without dropping eye contact and so avoid looking at her body, be it clothed or naked.

I later remembered another story about my hero, Richard Feynman, the Nobel prize winning physicist and bongo player who drew naked women. He told a story about how he had experienced the Japanese avoidance of the indiscreet glance while in that county.

He was staying in traditional Japanese hotel in Kyoto with his fellow physicist Abraham Pais and sharing a room.

He explained that there was a young woman who ran the bath for them in the morning before they got up. After she had left he had a bath, he then wrapped himself in a towel while Pais used the tub. As Abraham was stepping out of the water, 'sopping wet and completely nude' the young woman returned with their breakfast on a tray. She turned to Feynman, in his towel, bowed and said good morning and then turned to Prof Pais and with complete composure bowed and said good morning to him as well.

Feynman reported that Pais looked at him and said, 'We Americans are uncivilised compared to these folk.'

Feynman went on to explain that in America if a maid was delivering breakfast to two men in a room and with one wearing only a towel and the other standing there stark naked there would have been lots of screams and a big, embarrassing fuss. But the Japanese were used to public nakedness and were totally civilised about it

But what about the English? Was I about to meet a civilised lady who would be unfazed or would the rest of the household be rudely awakened by fuss and screaming?

I remember thinking why should our separate or possibly conjoined nakedness matter? Had we been a dog and bitch meeting on the corridor we would probably have sniffed each other's genitals to check if the female was on heat and the male desirable. But as a human I could foresee potential embarrassment, even shame, from my failure to dress. And if my lady visitor was also unclothed the embarrassment would be multiplied. She might not scream but she may not react in the disregarding way Feynman's Japanese maid had.

We would both be deprived of the masks we normally used to individualize ourselves and without uniforms to slot us into a social context. Because I was naked I had lost all the external references that clothes confer and all my male virtues and vices were available for her inspection. There were no props of class, economic, or social status to hide behind. My exposed body, with its unconstrained masculinity, proclaimed the fact that I was simply a naked ape. As such I was unable to walk towards a fellow human without making a sexual display. It is the price we naked apes have to pay for shedding our fur and walking upright.

I had no choice. My most secret self was about to be seen and judged by my lady guest. How I behaved while she was looking at me would have consequences for my social standing, my moral reputation and our ongoing friendship.

By going to the loo without bothering to dress I had voluntarily surrendered all claim to bodily privacy and tacitly accepted that anybody I might meet outside my own bedroom would not be invading my privacy if they stared at any, or every, part of my body, even those sexual parts normally considered private for a respectable academic.

As I had rapidly considered the range of actions available to me. I was most concerned about the infliction of my nakedness on a friend's privacy if I was about to meet our lady guest and she was respectably attired. My planned course of action if she was wearing a dressing gown was to apologize for being naked without warning her. If she indicated she wasn't offended then I wouldn't feel it was a breach of my privacy if she took the opportunity to stare at my body with blatant and undisguised curiosity. I just hoped she wouldn't giggle.

However, if she was clad in underwear, or completely nude then I would not feel I was making quite so big an intrusion upon her privacy. If she had chosen to wear little or no clothing she also had voluntarily accepted that she was prepared to be seen in whatever state of attire she has chosen for her trip to the loo. If it turned out she was unclothed than neither of us would have intruded on the other's private space as we would have engaged in a voluntary mutual surrender of any right to be offended by being stared at.

The sociologist Lois Shawver says that an etiquette of disregard protects us in situations where we feel it would be impolite to stare. This etiquette routinely protects people from curious stares in public toilets, shared changing rooms, saunas, nude beaches and medical encounters which involve disrobing in front of doctors and nurses of either sex.

Shawver asks is it possible for men and women to disregard each other's nakedness? She concludes that as long as there is no sexual intent in the encounter then it is. To support this view Shawver cites the example of medical investigations where we not only willingly remove our clothes at the request of a doctor who remains fully dressed, but we also allow them to touch even the most intimate parts of our bodies without embarrassment. This she says is because all medical staff are fully trained in the etiquette of disregard which involves chatting casually with the patients during the procedure and describing what is going on in a detached and professional manner. The trick it seems, is to separate the nudity from any sexual connotation. She also says that when observers disregard the sexuality of an encounter the embarrassment is reduced but adds that when the person with the undressed body behaves without evidence of embarrassment, i.e. with disregard, then this will encourage the observer to treat their nudity with a similar degree of disregard.

I deduced from this train of thought that I had to be careful to make no allusion to the sexual connotations and behave towards the naked lady as if she is not in any way an object of sexual interest.

The degree of embarrassment was in my gift. If I acted as though being naked was natural and normal, then there was every chance my lady guest would go along with it.

I would simply say 'Good Morning,' look the visiting lady in the eye, without a single glance downwards, and step gallantly to one side to let her pass, holding the bathroom door for her as a gentleman.

As the corridor came into my view I saw my guest, wearing just underwear. But it was the respectable Revd theologian who was sporting white boxer shorts. For a moment we stared at each other. I was buck naked and he was wearing just enough clothing to be considered respectable in the eyes of our wives, as his genitals were covered. We stood facing each other in the narrowest part of the corridor on either side of a small side table. We were both surprised. He, because he was not expecting to see anyone there and me because I was relieved I was not about to embarrass my lady guest. I followed the example of Feynman's Japanese maid.

'Good morning Jowett,' I said, in the tone of voice which suggested I was acknowledging him with a verbal court bow.

'Good morning,' he replied his voice as polite and controlled as mine. To anyone listening we might have been meeting for coffee in the senior common room.

My potential embarrassment evaporated the moment I saw he too was virtually naked. We had accidentally set up an implied mutual contract that we were both dressed in the nude. That moment I knew I was not going to embarrass his wife I felt quite comfortable in my bare skin. For a moment we stood and looked each other over. I saw an almost naked man, with a surprisingly rotund belly, who had discreetly covered his genitalia and backside to make the trip to the loo whilst I, being less cautious and not expecting to meet anyone, had everything hung out.

Despite our lack of uniforms, or social status symbols, we were as scrupulously polite as we exchanged greetings as if we had both been wearing suits and academic gowns. Neither of us mentioned our mutual state of undress as we both waited politely for the other to step forward. When neither of us did, we both moved forward together only to find we had to be very careful not to brush up against each other's bare skin, as between us we had plenty. We were both aware that our implied agreement to ignore our undress did not extent to permission to touch.

Chapter 5 The Male in All His Glory

When women pose thoughtfully and artistically - in nothing but their bare skin - they find themselves. They discover that they are truly alive. They become a Nude.
David Allio

It is embarrassing to admit just how curious I was becoming about what people's naked bodies look like. I was amazed at how simply taking up a pencil and sketch pad had given me a respectable license to stare at undressed people. But it was more than just a voyeur's charter. The revelation of seeing how powerful and emotionally moving Eileen's over-weight bulky naked presence had been when I saw her 'in pose' made me realise just how much of her spirit and joy in life had been hidden by her middle aged, practical dress. It is often said that women of a certain age become invisible. But if they remove their dowdy respectable wraps then the light of their human spirit shines out. 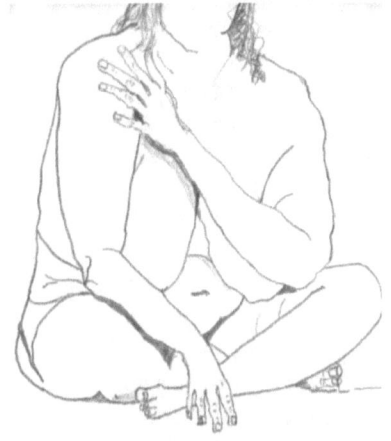 There is much to be learnt about the pleasure of drawing from the biblical instruction not to hide your light under a bushel.

Under Deborah's tuition I was starting to develop a freer style of drawing. For the first four weeks the class drew Eileen and I came to know her voluptuous curves and generous proportions quite well, then Deborah announced the following week we would be having a different model.

Alice, still retaining the bossy inquisitiveness of a primary school teacher, even though she was long retired, piped up. 'What's the new model like?'

'It's a man,' Deborah said. 'He's a friend of mine, a black Rasta Reggie Musician with really long dreadlocks.'

'I hope the rest of his manhood is really long too.' Alice said.

'This is not a peep show, Alice,' Deborah said her voice taking on a censorious primness. 'You should think about any model, irrespective of their gender, as simply a collection of shapes and curves which you are trying to capture onto paper. The model is not an object of desire, it is just something for you to draw, just like a bowl of fruit.'

'Like a pair of apples and banana?' asked Alice.

'If you don't behave yourself, and promise me you will be respectful towards Winston next week then I will ban you from the class,' said Deborah

'I promise to be respectful, even if I'm awestruck.' Alice said.

'You'd better be,' Deborah said.

As she was leaving Alice whispered to me. 'I'm looking forward to the chance to draw a fit young man.'

'I'm not sure I am,' I said.

'Why not?' she replied. 'He's got nothing you don't see every time to go to the loo.'

'But I'm worried he might be better equipped to piss higher up the wall.' I said.

'You men are all the same,' she said. 'All you worry about is the size of your willies. Life drawing is supposed to be a spiritual exercise in studying the human condition. Not a trial of length.'

With that we parted. I hung back to have a word with Deborah. I wondering how I was going to get on drawing a man. I admit I wasn't looking forward to staring at his groin no matter how big or small he was compared to me.

I suppose the gender of the model, the body type or pose should not have been an issue for me but I was still new to this game and so far I had only drawn naked women. As all Richard Feynman's published drawings of nudes were female I couldn't use his experience for inspiration.

'Some artists,' Deborah said, 'say that their understanding of the human form and its ability to hold a pose is enhanced by modelling themselves. Winston is an artist, so he's modelling to help him understand the strengths and limitation of his models.'

Deborah also added that since Winston had started modelling she'd seen a marked improvement in his life drawings.

'I hope that's not a hint.' I said.

She looked me up and down and then grinned. 'Nope, No way.' She said.' But here's a thought. artist Peter Steinhart suggests developing your drawing by focusing intently on your friends, saying he can't think of a better subject. He reckons it's easy to say to a friend: 'Hey, I'd like to draw you nude.' and assures us it will only feel weird for a few minutes.'

'Are you my friend?' I asked.

'No,' she said. 'I'm your teacher so don't ask. Try Alice.'

'I think she'd bite my head off,' I said.

'Now that would make an interesting still life. Like a study for St John the Baptist.' Deborah said as she ushered me out so she could lock up.

Is it that easy to pose nude even for a friend? You must remain motionless for long periods in positions that are as uncomfortable as they are humbling and revealing. Having your nakedness stared at with silent intensity, even by a friend, must be worrisome.

I have been a lecturer for all my working life, and have grown accustomed to people I don't know staring at me, but when I first gave public lectures being the centre of attention made me nervous. Over the years the troublesome overtones of being stared at by a large group have reduced, but I have the armour of my clothing and the respect for my status as a lecturer to help me. I learned long ago that the best way to relate to an audience, and engage with them, is to successively make eye-contact with individuals, so that they can feel as if I am interacting personally with each and every one of them.

But an artist does not engage in two-way eye contact, an artist stares. And, as I had noticed with my fellow artists, their stare whilst engaged in the process of drawing, is cold, analytical and probing. It is uncomfortable for a clothed person to be the subject of such intense observation. I see this by the way my clothed friends start to wriggle when they realize I am drawing them. How much worse would such an intense stare feel if they were naked? I can't get away from the idea that the act of undressing and being stared at naked, even by a friend, has inherent sexual overtones. My early morning experience had made me fully aware of just how stressful being caught without my pants can be.

Soon I would see how Winston handled being closely scrutinised in the buff.

I arrived at the class early as I wanted to see Winston arrive. I was getting interested in the contrast between the clothed individual and nude model. Two things struck me about him when I first saw him. The striking plethora of plats which adorned his hair and the hippy scruffiness of his clothing. Here, I thought, as he ambled in, is one laid back, cool dude.

'Is he the new model?' Alice said as she followed him into the room. 'He looks fit.'

Deborah glared at her.

'He must spend quite a bit of time in the gym.' Alice added, unabashed.

She was right he did look fit, he walked with the casual arrogance of a man who was comfortable in own body and who didn't look at all nervous about stripping down to his skin to stand in front of a group of mature women, Deborah and couple of elderly guys..

I could see Alice was looking forward to drawing all his manly attributes. She had an intense look about her that reminded me of other lady teachers, from my past whom I had witnessed reacting to naked males disporting themselves before them. This happened more years ago than I care to admit to. Let's just say it was in the past, which we all know is a completely different country and could never happen nowadays. But I'll tell you about it anyway.

At the age of eleven, having failed the Eleven-plus I was sent to an all-boys Secondary Modern School which had four graded forms of entry. I wasn't even good enough to make the top class, an Alpha-stream, I was put into the second stream, incongruously called the A-stream. This was five years before I realised I had a tremendous, although rather autistic, talent for numbers, went to technical college and won an exhibition to a college at one of the older universities to read mathematics. At eleven, while still a normal dullard, I was expected to take part in Physical Education and play games. And this involved public nudity.

PE was a perpetual threat to me between the ages of 11 to 16 years, after which I joined the sixth form and no longer had to take part. Physical Education was compulsory and involved changing out of school uniform (white shirt and school tie, blazer, grey short trousers, grey socks and black shoes) into PE kit that consisted of white tee-shirt, white shorts and pumps. PE lessons were taken twice a week by, a teacher I will call, Mr Porter and took place in the school hall. The class changed into their PE kit in the cloakroom. This was a narrow room with four rows of coat hooks with wooden benches underneath them which ran length ways from the door to the windows. Each boy in the class would go to his own hook, where he usually hung his coat and his PE bag as he came into school, and change into his PE kit.

During the dark days of winter the cloakroom always smelt of damp gabardine with an added dank overtone of unwashed boy. When a PE lesson was timetabled the class would line up outside the cloakroom. Mr Porter would arrive and tell us to change and then go along the corridor to the school hall. We would go to our peg, take down our PE bag, which was usually a draw string cloth bag. Take out our shorts and tee-shirt. Remove our uniforms, hanging all our clothes on the hook with our coat and then put on the tee-shirt, shorts and pumps. The hall, which we also used for morning assemblies, was well heated. The PE equipment, the mats, the climbing ropes, the benches, the vaulting horse and pommel horse were all stored at the back of the hall so the first job was to get out the equipment and set it up. We would then spend half an hour, climbing, scrambling and jumping about under Mr Porter's stern gaze.

Once a week the class also had a double period of games, which meant football in winter, and cricket in summer. For games there was a proper changing room. In winter, games kit consisted of shorts, sports shirt in the school colours, football boots and thick socks. When my mother packed my games kit I wondered why she put a towel and some soap in a plastic box in the bag. The first time the sodden, muddy class trooped back into school buildings I understood.

Mr Porter hustled us into the changing room, turned on the communal shower and told us all to strip. That was the first time I had ever had a shower, at home we only had a bath, and it was the first time since my grandmother had bathed me as a child that I had washed my naked body in public. The communal shower was an eye-opening surprise. I didn't like games as I was no good at football and didn't like getting cold and muddy.

I liked the hot showers, although I would have preferred not to have had to push and shove with forty other naked boys to get under one of the five shower heads. It was crowded, up close and intimate in those communal showers. But someone once said 'you never really know your friends until you see them naked.'

This was certainly true of my friends at secondary school. My closest friends were in the same class as me and we regularly saw each other stripping off to change into PE kit and for longer periods as we showered together and shared a bar of soap. I realise now that at school my friends, my enemies and even some of my teachers knew me very well.

Twice a week I stripped off in front of all my classmates and Mr Porter. Then once a week I shared a shower head with at least half dozen, while the other three dozen kept looking and commentating on how much pubic hair was growing round my willie and showing me how much hairier than me they were. What made this experience completely egalitarian was that if our games period was at the end of the school day, Mr Porter would leave us to shower for about 5 minutes. Then he would come in, still in his games kit, carrying a track suit, and order us all out from under the water jets to dry ourselves and get dressed. While we were dressing he would strip off and shower himself. And nobody ever accused him of lacking pubic hair.

What I soon realised was that once your school mates have seen you naked, they've seen you naked. The same is true for you of them. The suspense is over. They know all your flaws and you know theirs, once you've seen their willie, their belly and their backside it's done. You know whose willie is biggest, who has the biggest balls, whose lower belly has the most hair and who has the fattest backside. But you're still in the same class, you still have the same PE and games lessons and you're going to have to shower with them all again before the week's ended. Neither you or them will look different the second time they see you naked (or the third or the hundredth), so there will be no more surprises. If you have the biggest willie in week 1 you'll probably still have the biggest willie at the end of term (assuming there are no sudden surges in growth among your classmates). However, once you've been naked with your classmates you can walk around naked as much as you want without anything new being revealed. Certainly it was a real shock the first time we all had to get naked together, and an even bigger shock the first time we all crushed into the showers *en masse*, But the experience probably made sure I didn't have a lifetime of neuroses like my mother, who wouldn't even let my father see her naked. Certainly this communal nudity came as a surprise at first but after a couple of weeks there was another shock in store for me.

Mr Porter was very strict about doing everyone doing PE. Just how strict he was became apparent about three weeks into term when one boy, who I will call Noah Flood, forgot to bring his gym kit in one Monday morning. The class was timetabled for PE in the afternoon and he realised he had forgotten his gym bag. At play time he was wandering round telling anyone who'd listen that he would get out of doing PE as he hadn't got any kit to wear. I must confess to feeling that he had worked out a really good wheeze to get out of PE and perhaps I could try it next week, it was too late for this week as my freshly washed tee-shirt and shorts were already hung from my coat peg waiting for me.

The class were all wondering what would happen. We knew that Flood wouldn't be allowed to do PE in his uniform and he hadn't got any gym kit to put on. We wondered if he would be caned or put in detention for forgetting his kit, but we were all quite sure he wouldn't be joining us in the hall for our physical exertions.

Me and my mate Howard were already changed. I knocked around with Howard because his coat peg was right next to mine. Noah Flood came in. His coat peg was two down from us, and he hung up his blazer before taking off his shoes and socks. Most of the others had already gone off to the hall.

'What're you doing here?' I asked.

'I've got to get changed.' he said.

'What into?' Howard asked.

'Nothing,' Noah said, he didn't look very happy.

'Nothing?' Howard echoed, his eyes widening in alarm.

'Nothing,' Noah confirmed, pulling his shorts and underpants down. He took his shirt off and stood before us bollock-naked.

'I'm ready,' he said as he pushed past us towards the corridor. Howard and I quickly hitched up our shorts, mainly for the feeling of security it gave us, and set off after him, hardly able to believe our eyes as the muscles in his naked backside bobbed and flexed as he walked along. The school was built around an open lawned-quadrangle, with science labs along the east side, classrooms along the south, woodwork shops along the west and the music room, the art room and the hall on the north side. The corridors were glass covered tunnels around the side of the quad, which had a path across from the hall to the staff room, which only teachers were allowed to use. To get from the cloak room to the hall we had to walk along the north corridor past the art room.

We only had one women teacher, who I shall call Mrs Richmond. It was unlucky for Noah that she happened to be walking from the music room, passed the hall towards the art room. Howard and I both saw her before she noticed Flood. It was rather a cartoon moment. She stopped dead and her eyes bulged as she stared at Flood's full frontal display of teenage indecency.

'Flood!' she thundered. 'Why are you naked on a public corridor?'

Howard and I rushed passed as quickly as we could and having reached the safety of the hall door, with Mrs Richmond's back towards us, we turned to watch. Noah was frantically trying to hide his sexual parts with both hands.

'I forgot...t...t... my PE kit Miss, ' he stuttered, his face glowing as red as a traffic light. 'And Mr Porter told me I had to change into what I'd brought.'

'Stand up straight, put your hands on your head, and stop playing with yourself, boy' She ordered. 'You're disgusting.'

Flood stood up straight and put his hands on his head.

'Look,' whispered Howard, staring at Noah's willie. 'he's twitching. Do you think he's going to get a hard on?'

'I hope so,' I said. I wasn't quite sure what Howard meant by a hard on, but I was enjoying Flood's humiliation. It would never matter in future that he had more pubic hair than me. I'd seen him being forced to show his willie to Mrs Richmond on the school corridor and I would be able to laugh about it whenever he took his pants off for weeks.

'In future make sure you bring your kit.' She said, staring at his still twitching willie, which seemed to have a will of its own and was refusing to keep still. 'I never want to see you flaunting yourself in the nude on this corridor again. Is that quite clear?'

'Yes Miss,' Flood said, very quietly, looking at the ground.

'Now get out of my sight at once.' she said.

Flood dropped his arms to his sides, keeping them well away from his groin and walked passed Mrs Richmond towards the hall. As she turned to watch him go she saw Howard and me.

'Stop gawping you two.' she ordered. 'Or you'll be in detention for weeks and I'll confiscate your PE kit.'

As we didn't want to be stripped of our gym kit, we quickly backed into the hall, closely followed by Flood who was promptly greeted with a cacophony of cat-calls and wolf-whistles.

The rest of the PE lesson went pretty much as normal, Mr Porter simply ignored the fact the Flood was naked. And he didn't notice when Jeff Taylor grabbed Flood by the balls and squeezed them hard as Noah was climbing up the rope which Jeff had hold of, not even when Flood yelped.

'No talking,' he said. 'Get up that rope Flood and stop messing about!

'Look how his willie flips and flops about when he runs?' Howard whispered as we all ran round the hall ten times at the end of lesson. 'It's like a conker string dangling between his legs. Do you think mine would wave about like that if I took my shorts off?'

'No,' I said. 'It's far too short to wave at all.'

After that whenever Noah stripped off for the communal shower after games the whole class would whistle at him and call out 'Here comes Floud the Nuude.'

In the third year (we were Class 3A now) our class of thirteen year old boys got a new probationary teacher for geography whom I will call Miss Ridgway. Unlike Mrs Richmond, Miss Ridgway. was young and pretty and fresh out of college. Instead of shapeless tweeds she wore tight sweaters, various miniskirts with a selection of kinky boots, (after all this was the nineteen sixties) and was in the habit of sitting on top of the teacher's desk with her legs crossed when she was teaching us geography. We paid close attention to her, and Jeff Taylor reckoned he could see her knickers from where he had to sit on the front row, especially if he dropped his pencil and had to crouch down to pick it up. (Mr Brownley, our form teacher, had made him sit at the front so he couldn't mess about in class. I wondered if I should mess about a bit more so that I could get a seat at the front. Although I wouldn't admit to Jeff Taylor I'd never ever seen any girl's knickers let alone a real woman's knickers up a mini skirt.)

We all liked talking to Miss Ridgeway and she told us that she believed in something called Women's Lib and that a woman could do anything a man could. We laughed at that idea, but not when she was listening. Somehow Jeff Taylor found out her first name was Doreen.

The class still had its twice weekly PE lessons with Mr Porter and games were now timetabled for the last double period on a Thursday. We were all quite used to Mr Porter having a shower after us at the end of the games session but we were quite surprised when he told us that from the following week, Miss Ridgeway would be helping out with games. Sure enough the following Thursday she was out on the pitch with us acting as linesman. Mr Porter, who was always the referee, wore a football shirt and shorts, but Miss Ridgeway wore a tight fitting track suit and football boots. She arrived for the lesson already wearing her tracksuit and met us on the field. She didn't come into the changing room. Then one week Mr Porter was taken ill.

When it was announced in morning assembly that Mr Porter was off sick we all thought that games and PE would be cancelled. But instead we were told that Miss Ridgeway would be taking over Mr Porter's lessons for the next two weeks. I was extremely disappointed because I'd hoped that games would be cancelled and that I could do something more interesting inside, like reading a good book on mathematics, doing some interesting sums or practising playing Mozart with the recorder group. But games it was to be.

Miss Ridgeway met us outside the changing room and told us that we would be playing football as usual and she would be referee. We went in and started to change. By now we were all in the habit of stripping naked, hanging up our uniforms and then putting on our sports kit. Jeff Taylor was as usual playing the clown. As soon as he undressed he started dancing up and down to make his willie whirl about.

He was still bounding around naked and yelling like a monkey when, we heard someone approach the door.

Howard was just putting his left leg into his shorts as Miss Ridgeway came in.

'What's all that noise?' she yelled. Howard quickly pulled his shorts up but Jeff Taylor was standing in the middle of the shower area gyrating his willie shouting, 'Look at this, Look at this I'm an aeroplane.'

'GET YOUR KIT ON AT ONCE!' Miss Ridgeway thundered. Jeff froze. Miss Ridgeway was not wearing her usual cover-all tracksuit, instead she had on a football shirt, over a pair of navy gym knickers with football boots. She had knee-length socks to finish off her outfit. As Jeff stared along the full length of her legs he suddenly remembered he was naked and quickly reached down and covered himself with his hands.

'NOW!' she said. Jeff scuttled to his peg, still hiding behind his hands and turned his back towards her as he quickly pulled on his shorts. The rest of the class quickly all finished dressing and lined up by the door.

Miss Ridgeway turned out to be an energetic referee. She was dashing everywhere on the field and was quick at dodging out of the way of oncoming players. But the field was muddy and the ground slippery. More than once she slipped and fell full length in the mud. By the end of the game her kit was wet, muddy and clinging while she, and her long, long legs, was just as caked with mud as the rest of us.

'In you all go and shower,' she said. 'You've got five minutes.'

We boys, being boys spent at least a couple of minutes discussing how her shape had become more obvious when her shirt was plastered with wet muck, as we took off our own mud soaked kit. Then we struggled and pushed for the best spots under the shower as we sluiced away the mire from our legs and arms. The five minutes went quickly and everybody was still in the shower when the door to the changing room opened and Miss Ridgeway walked in carrying her tracksuit and a towel. She was wearing a one-piece bathing suit which showed traces of mud and every curve. She must have been wearing it under her football kit. Despite her mud plastered legs and arms, I thought she looked as good as any Miss World contestant. I gave a wolf-whistle under my breath, as I was naked I was far too afraid to do it out loud, Wow, I thought. This is better than old Porter and his hairy old willie any day.

'Get dressed now boys,' she said. 'Shower time's over.' The crowd of naked boys took flight like a startled flock of frightened chickens at the sight of a fox. They rushed to wrap towels round their waists and crawl back into their protective uniforms as quickly as damp skin would permit. Never since that first games session, when we all realised we would have strip naked in front of the whole class and its teacher, had there been such a collective outbreak of modest demeanour amid the boys of Class 3A

Realising that Miss Ridgeway had already seen anything I had to hide, I decided I wouldn't make a fool of myself like Jeff had by trying to conceal strategic bits of my body. I finished sluicing off the soap and so was the last boy to leave the shower.

I felt I could actually feel Miss Ridgeway's eyes looking at my nakedness and the knowledge I was being looked by an attractive woman gave me a fluttery feeling in my stomach. I stood, a streaming tableau of indecision, trying to furtively stare at her whilst also pretending I wasn't. She walked towards me. 'Hurry up, out of the shower and get dressed Cowley' she said. 'I need a wash too.'

As I stood next to Howard, drying myself, Miss Ridgeway put her towel and track suit down on a spare bench, took out a bottle of shampoo, stood under the water flow and started to wash her hair. You could almost hear the jaws of the class clanging open as they stared at her. She seemed quite oblivious to our covert attention as she washed away the mud of the playing fields.

'Do you think she's going to take off her swimming costume to dry herself?' Howard whispered. 'I've never seen a naked woman. I won't know where to look.'

Miss Ridgeway finished washing, turned off the water and reached for her towel.

'Right Class. Off you go,' she said, pointing at the door. 'Home time.'

We reluctantly trooped out, all watching her as we did.

'And close the door as you go,' she called after us. And we did. When the door opened and she came out she was carrying the swimsuit and the towel, and wearing the tracksuit.

Now for the first time in many years I about to share an intimate space with a naked male with whom I might feel compelled to draw comparisons. I didn't really want to revert to that old school boy competition of who's got the biggest wille, even if I would be the only one to really know, so to avoid the issue I carefully positioned myself to draw a back view.

Winston came out in his robe, agreed with Deborah that he would sit on a low stool and pose with his hands clasped behind his back. Alice settled herself in front of him while I took a seat directly behind him.

He stood with his back to me, dropped his robe and sat down in pose. His tightly platted dreadlocks hung down below his waist as you can see from the drawing I did of him. I had never seen Alice's gaze quite so quite so intense as she drew his ventral aspect. She kept stopping to measure by sighting with her pencil, and as she did she kept winking at me. I ignored her and concentrated on depicting his dorsal view.

Deborah came round and looked at my drawing.

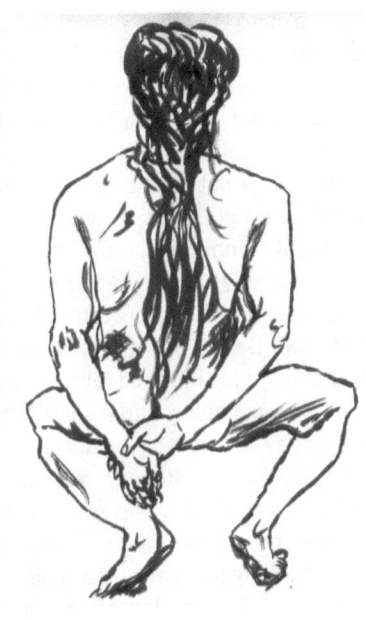

'Not too bad.' She said, 'for the next pose I'll get Winston to sit with his hands on his knees so you can try a front view.'

I didn't explain that I had been had been avoiding settling down to gaze at Winston's willie as the thought of doing so and being caught by Deborah 'taking an unhealthy interest in another boy's privates' had given me a flashback to my mother saying exactly that when she caught me in the bathroom of the family flat with my trousers round my ankles staring at the almost hairless genitalia of my primary school pal David Founder, who also had his trousers round his ankles.

We were about eight years old at the time and had been allowed to play with a clockwork model boat in the bath. David had felt the need to have a tinkle into the toilet. When he'd finished he'd looked over his shoulder and said.

'Would you like to see my rupert?'

Now I wasn't sure what a rupert was so I sort of half nodded my head.

'If you pull your shorts down I'll pull mine down too,' he said. 'You go first.'

As I've mentioned before, nakedness was not considered a desirable state in my mother's house, except when I was about to get into a bath full of water. As I was stood next to a bath full of water I reasoned that perhaps dropping my trousers would be acceptable, as the bath full of water would make the nakedness all right. I just wore short khaki trousers without underwear in those distant, innocent summer days so I unclipped my elastic snake buckle belt, undid the buttons of my fly and let my shorts fall. David looked at my tiny hairless penis. Then he undid his belt and let his trousers fall. He wasn't wearing anything under his shorts either. It was a warm day in mid-August and neither of us were wearing shirts, so with our trousers lowered we were effectively naked. I had never before seen any other naked body than my own, and I had only really seen that during my weekly bath night.

'I've got some hair growing round my rupert,' David said proudly, pointing at his lower belly. I looked closely, and my eyesight was sharp in the those days, but I could only just about see a few blond hairs. However, I was jealous, as it was more than I had. I was smooth as a hard-boiled egg.

'Only just,' I said hoping to stop him telling everyone in our class I was deformed under my trousers. That was when my mother burst in to check we were all right. I was given the strap on my bare legs and David was sent home.

When Deborah adopted a sharp tone of voice she reminded me of my mother. That sixty year old memory had burned itself into my psyche and even though my intellect told me I was not only allowed, I was expected, to look at Winston's rupert my emotional mind was expecting a telling off.

Deborah was looking at me and waiting.

'I don't mind drawing his back,' I said, hoping to avoid having to sit next to Alice as Deborah pushed me to measure and draw Winston's manly assets. If Alice's exaggerated display of measuring and the length of his dreadlocks were a general indicator then I didn't want to know how big he might be. I felt I might put myself at risk of an immediate inferiority complex and Alice was bound to try to draw me into comparative assessments with myself. She had that sort of glint in her eye.

'Move round to his side Maurice,' Deborah said. 'I want to see how you handle a male torso.'

I almost said that I didn't want to handle a male torso, but I didn't want Deborah to give me a lecture about the asexual beauty of the nude body of either sex. As far I was concerned nude females were less threatening than naked males. I had had my fill of pressing male flesh in the communal showers, but back then then I could always stand next to Howard, and look pretty good. I wasn't sure I was going to be comfortable sitting staring at Winston's groin. However Deborah insisted.

She set Winston up in a seated pose and I moved round to the side, but not too far round, as I didn't want to obstruct Alice's viewpoint.

I managed to do an oblique view of the pose which saved me from having to draw any of his obviously male bits. As his dreadlocks were out of sight down his back and his legs modestly shielded his groin area I thought my drawing look quite decorous. As I sat back admiring it Deborah came round to inspect our efforts. She looked first at Alice's sketch.

'Not bad,' she said, 'But you may have slightly exaggerated this feature' She pointed down at somewhere in the middle of Alice's drawing, which was angled away from me so I couldn't see exactly what she meant, but from Alice's extended measuring efforts I could make a guess. She came over and looked at my drawing.

'Maurice,' she said. 'Are you deliberately avoiding drawing Winston's penis?'

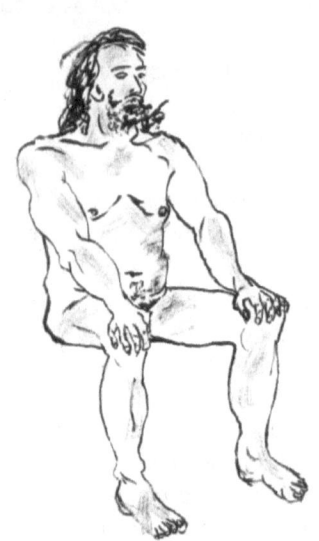

'I didn't want to get in Alice's way,' I said, 'So I sat slightly to the side, and you did say that we should try and draw exactly what we could see.'

'In that case,' she said, 'I'll make it easier for you.' She looked at Winston, who was wearing his robe and stretching. 'Can you do a thirty minute standing pose. Please?' she asked.

'Sure Debby. Just ask for what you want,' Winston agreed affably. He stood up, dropped his robe and clasped his left elbow with his right hand.

'That' a nice angular shape,' Deborah said. 'But would you mind turning to face Maurice?'

'Whatever you say, Debby.' Winston agreed. He turned to face me. And grinned all over his face. Visions of Jeff Taylor prancing naked around the communal shower and whirling his willie like a propeller, in front of a livid Miss Ridgeway flashed before my eyes. I fought them down and realised

Winston wasn't much bigger than I was. My fears began to ebb away.

'Look closely, measure carefully and get the proportions right.' Deborah said. 'The model is only a normal person without clothing, and if you are going to learn to draw the human form you have to spend time looking at every aspect of it. It's not a sexual thing. It's simply a set of planes, curves and shadows you have to translate into lines on your paper.' She looked at Winston. 'Can you hold that for thirty minutes?'

Sure can, dead easy,' Winston agreed.

'Right class! Get on with your drawing.' Deborah ordered. I did as I was told.

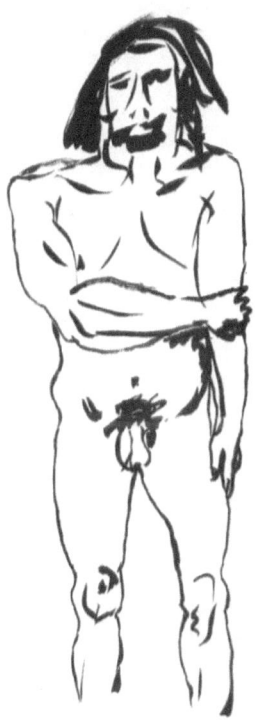

'See, it wasn't that hard.' Deborah said when we had finished. 'Life modelling is not about sex or modesty, it's about knowing how to look at the most familiar three dimensional object in the world and then translate that vision into two dimensions.'

'Yes Miss,' I said.

'Maurice,' she said looking me in the eye and holding her stare. 'To allow yourself be offended by the visual appearance of another person is prejudice, akin to racism. Even if you are afraid of being suspected of prurient motives if you stare at another man's penis. His right to be uncovered, should hold precedence over your right to be irrationally afraid of looking at his sexual organ. You are learning to be an artist and tonight you are learning that you must never be afraid to look at any part of any human body.'

'Certainly, Miss,' I said, holding her gaze. 'In future I will always look closely at whatever you place before me to draw.'

If only she had known me in my younger summers I feel she would have been less worried about me.

I'm glad to hear that,' she said. 'Because I'm going to ask Winston to do a another standing pose and I want you to draw a frontal middle torso of him, and I want you to carefully observe and draw his penis.'

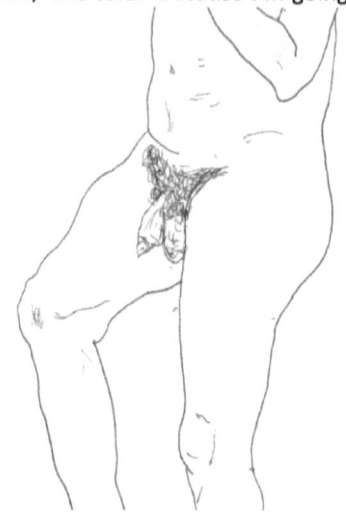

'Yes, Miss' I said with a deep gulp which she pretended not to notice.

I reached for my pencil and carefully sharpened it, avoiding Alice's amused stare as I did so. I wondered if I should lick the sharpened tip and smile at her, but decided against it as I was supposed to doing this for the sake of Art, not to score points off Alice.

And here is the detailed drawing I did of Winstan's lower body with no detail overlooked.

When the session finished Winston got dressed and had a few words with Deborah. As he was leaving I caught his eye.

'Thanks for modelling,' I said. 'You were really still. How easy do you find holding a pose?'

'It's not too difficult,' he said. 'I just enjoy the beauty of stillness.'

'Deborah said you're an artist.' I said.

'Yes, I am,' he said.

'Is that why you also model, to understand how your model feels?' I said.

'Let me be honest,' he said with a twinkle in his eye. 'I do model to help artists and art students develop their skills, and it does help me understand what sorts of poses a model can hold. But the main appeal is being nude in front of artists of the opposite sex. Debby actually pays me to allow her, and her class of main female artists, to study my naked body.'

Chapter 6 Pushing the Limits of Exposure

Posing nude gives me a chance to explore beyond what is typically acceptable. Posing nude lets me mess with the borders between public and private. Posing nude lets me consider my desire for a certain kind of attention. And it lets me confront the idea that I want that kind of attention.
— Kathleen Rooney Writer and Model

It is the ultimate test of an individual's body confidence to stand naked and display their personal sexual features to the detailed scrutiny of a roomful of strangers. It requires enormous trust, to render themselves so vulnerable.

As I was drawing the intimate details of Winston's nether regions I found myself empathising with this human male who had agreed pose naked for an extended drawing session. He had to trust me to respect his vulnerability, but I had to learn how to stare at his body in a way which I would normally only do to a sexual partner. I might have glanced briefly at my naked female friends when meeting them by accident but I would never think of staring at their groin for half an hour. It was this intrusive almost sexual gaze which Deborah had spotted I was struggling to achieve when drawing my first male nude. I had learned to stare at a naked woman in order to suck in every detail of her body, but it felt extremely uncomfortable to be looking at a naked man with what would normally be erotic intensity. This was why Deborah had pushed me to do a full frontal drawing of Winston.

Winston said posing was rather like meditating. He explained that to model properly he had to stay focused on every aspect of his body, to keep it in the same position for long periods of time. Even if he was enjoying the attention it must still have felt strange to be observed in such intense detail over such a long period without any chance to hide or turn away. He had no chance to maintain a false mask over his soul during such profound and prolonged exposure.

I couldn't help thinking what would I have revealed if I had been the model? What would have escaped from that great store of things I normally conceal beneath the protective shell of my clothing?

I had already learned that life drawing was easiest when the model was a silent complete-stranger. In such a case I could accept the model as just a human-like object placed there for me to draw. I could project the best aspects of my own soul onto what was a blank and silent canvass. I had already discovered it is much harder to draw someone I know intimately.

The problem was that I would normally have a two-way relationship with them which is expressed through non-verbal signals. When I drew them, this continual exchange of glances had to stop. I stared intently at them yet demanded that they remain still and passive. It was hard for my model to be under my gaze and not respond. Yet if they managed to remain motionless their soul would shine out and I felt I might be sometimes capturing what I knew to be there. But it was extremely hard work for the model. A joyful recreation for me became a tiring and exacting chore for my voluntary models and soon my family avoided sitting for me. I ended up only able to sketch them when they felt asleep or as quick gesture poses captured in a few lines before they noticed me staring again.

This problem arises because to draw well the artist needs to stare in silence and all human instincts tell us that silent staring is an act of aggression. As an experiment I tried getting a friend to sit for me, clothed of course. I tried to draw my old college friend Bernie, while she was sitting quietly. Within a few minutes she was getting uncomfortable and starting to squirm. Clearly my silent staring disturbed her.

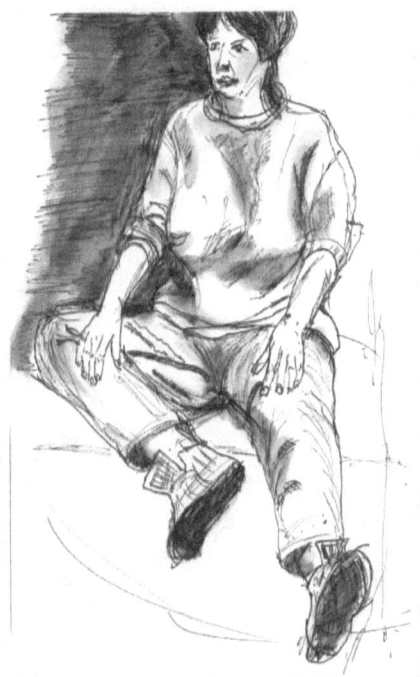

However I discovered that posed draped sketch with its rapid scribbles was much more lifelike because I knew what shapes lay underneath the clothed outline. It was true that life drawing was helping me to draw humans that looked human.

But how does a naked model, who is so much more exposed, manage not to squirm under the insistent silent stares which are needed to collect enough detail to draw them? Did the disciplined ritual of the life drawing studio, which I was learning from Deborah, make it easier?

It seems strange that a naked model can be cocooned within a zone of privacy but that is what happens in a life studio once the model removes their robe and steps into pose. As the art critic John Berger said. 'Nudity is a form of dress.' And once the model is nude on the stand everyone else is respectful of their role. The model is private because all the artists looking at them consider they are not naked, but displaying a nude body for the sake of Art. Their privacy is something that is gifted on them by those who observe them. The observers create the model's feelings of privacy and value.

Let me illustrate this by telling another little story about the practical workings of privacy I discovered by accident. This happened when I was staying in my small holiday bungalow with my wife and Bernie, the female friend from my college days who squirms if I draw her fully clothed.

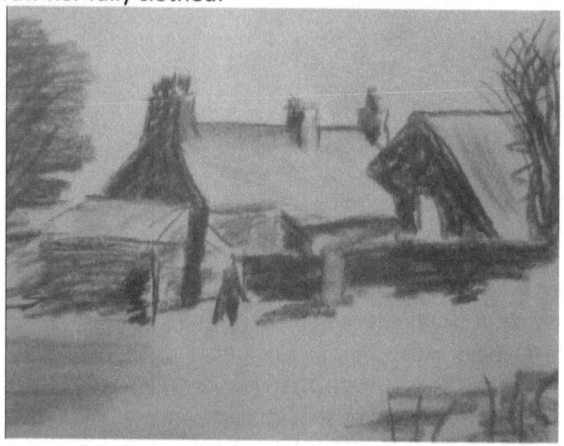

As I have mentioned before, the living room opens on to the same corridor as both bedrooms, the living room and the bathroom, so it is easy to wander in and out of any of the rooms.

Early one morning my wife received a phone call about an accident to one our daughter's friends. Apparently the details of the accident had been reported on the BBC news. Having just been roused from sleep my wife was nude when she got up to take the call but as we had a house guest, and she had to go onto the corridor to answer the landline, she slipped into a night dress. She left our bedroom door open, while she talked on the phone. Wanting to know more about the incident she told me to look up the news item on the internet, using a computer that was set up on a table in the corner of our bedroom.

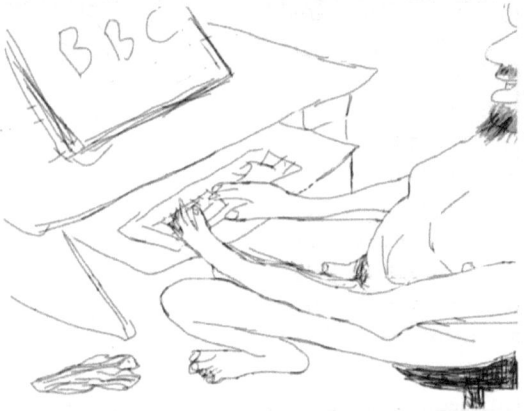

I usually do what my wife tells me, being well aware this helps ensure a more peaceful life so I got out of bed and turned on the computer. My wife called out to Bernie to come through so she also could read the news from the web. It was then that my wife noticed I had no clothes on. This was not surprising as I had just got out of bed. She ordered me to 'put something on'. Following her instructions, I stood up from the computer with the intention of moving towards the underpants I had discarded the night before, to put them on. However as I started to

79

move from the keyboard she changed her mind and said. 'Get that news item up first.'

While I was doing as she had instructed me, Bernie tapped on the open bedroom door and asked 'May I come in?'

My wife called out 'yes', so Bernie came in, and stood beside to me, watching as I called up the relevant information on the screen. Then my wife realised that I still had nothing on.

'I told you to put something on,' she said, forgetting that she had also told me to finish calling up the news item when I had moved towards my pants. I decided not to protest. It seemed pointless, as I was not only outnumbered by women I was the only nude person in the room. And who listens to the views of a naked man?

Bernie was wearing a white off the shoulder night gown, that she had obviously thrown on to come through to our bedroom, and was clearly naked underneath. I know, from past encounters with her in the corridor whilst visiting the loo in the early morning, that she not only sleeps naked but doesn't usually bother dressing just to go to the bathroom.

'Don't mind me,' she said. My wife glared at me so I moved to the side, squeezing passed Bernie, to let the women read the screen. I took the opportunity to pull on yesterday's underpants and, now minimally covered, I returned to the computer driving seat.

For the next quarter of an hour I operated the computer for the two women, carrying out web searches as they asked. I was still functionally naked, as the slender, clinging slip pants hid little of my anatomy and concealed no surprises as both women had stared at me while I picked them up from the floor and put them on. The women were wearing nothing under the flimsy night gowns, which they had thrown on quickly. But neither of them seemed be bothered about their unsubstantial clothing or their lack of undies, indeed I was now the only person in the room wearing panties which should have given me the moral high ground, but it didn't. I suspect I felt the most exposed of the three of us, but once I had donned a tiny scrap of white cotton my wife accepted me as decent.

Bernie didn't seem to care either way. So it would appear that the minimum amount of clothing necessary to be considered respectable in the company of more than one lady is a brief dhoti. Yet I

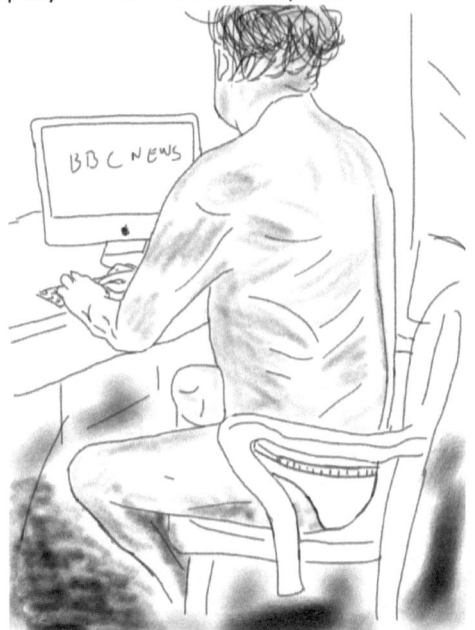

felt less comfortable wearing skimpy underwear than I had felt naked. To put on yesterday's used underwear with my old college friend watching me, made me feel a lack of privacy. I didn't mind her seeing me naked but I didn't want her to see me pulling on soiled underpants. Perhaps that feeling of shame was what my wife intended when she made me to do just that.

Underpants carry more symbolic power than any other garment. Sociologist Sarah Phillips pointed out underpants are personal and intimate, we do not share them, and we only reveal them selectively to intimate associates. Research by anthropologists James Henslin and Mae Biggs found that woman undressing for a gynaecological examination were far more worried about the doctor seeing their panties than they were about them viewing and touching their vaginas. They found that whilst undressing, alone in the examination room, the women hide their panties either in their handbag, in the pocket of their coat or under a sweater or skirt. It was rare for any of the women interviewed to leave their panties exposed to the doctor's gaze.

Wearing only yesterday's soiled knickers, in the company of two women, completely commando, under their insubstantial night-dresses, made me feel I was showing a far more intimate view of myself, than my naked body had disclosed.

The moral of this simple social encounter is that nakedness is not always an invasion of privacy between trusting friends. But social interaction, when unclothed, can cause a change in the rules of engagement which is outside the control of the naked person. This difference in attitude is captured in the semantic difference between being naked and being nude. Let me explain.

To any person accidently walking into a life drawing class the model is 'naked'. The difference between being nude and being naked is a matter of mutual perception and agreement. If you have voluntarily removed your clothes and the person observing you has accepted, and agreed to, your lack of clothing then you are nude. If you are seen by someone who has not agreed to look at your unclothed body you are naked. This means that difference between being naked and being nude is a phenomenon which is mediated by the observers and is totally out of the control of the unclothed individual. I will explain in the context of the scenario I described above.

Whist turning on the computer for my wife I was nude but when my friend Bernie walked in I suddenly became naked in the view of my wife, even though I was nude as far Bernie was concerned. In my wife's eyes the presence of another woman turned what had been perfectly acceptable nudity into unacceptable nakedness. But neither my body or my perception of myself had changed in any way. But I must explain what I mean by my perception of myself.

My self-perception involves my emotions, my bodily reactions to stimuli and my reason. It is the narrative I create which links my actions now, with my actions in the past and gives me a sense of continuity that I am a coherent individual despite the passage of time. As the molecules and atoms of my body are continually changing I cannot be exactly the same conglomerate of materials that I was twenty years ago, and yet I feel that the me of twenty years ago is still the me of today. As a natural organism I experience sensations which I interpret to infer information about the outside world. Within my mind I create expectations about the future and store memories about the past. I have desires, some of which arise from my mind and some of which arise from my body. I have needs, for warmth, for food and for air to breath, but I also have interactive needs where I need to feel that I have some purpose and value as an individual. Sometimes my needs and inclinations run against the dictates of my reason and I do things which are not necessarily always

83

logical. I sometimes have an urge to be noticed and be the centre of attention.

When my wife invited my old college girlfriend into our bedroom while I was not wearing clothes my wife's evaluation of me changed from acceptably nude to indecently exposed. My wife was reacting against my male inclination, as succinctly explained by Winston, to display my reproductive masculinity to a woman who was not my wife, with my wife also present. It can be argued that this was not a sensible way for a respectable academic to behave, even though Bernie came into the bedroom at my wife's invitation while I was sitting at the computer, innocently nude. I could not be accused of exhibitionism because I had not rushed to remove my clothing simply because Bernie came in. I was naturally and normally naked before she entered at the invitation of my wife. Logic says my wife should have considered me innocently nude under such circumstances, but she didn't. Whilst I realised intellectually that even inadvertent revealing of my genitals was not technically polite behaviour, my body, which has evolved as a mechanism of sexual reproduction, wanted to show itself off to a woman who was not averse to viewing it. I knew my old friend Bernie was not afraid of using what might be called 'the gaze' or 'the indiscreet glance'.

To an outside observer my failure to dress before the entry of our lady visitor, no matter what deep and highly personal desires it was satisfying in the privacy of my inner self, can only be viewed as making a latent sexual offer to another female who had come within range. I was inviting disapproval, if not from Bernie, then certainly from my wife by exposing myself to a female friend in her presence. On later reflection it occurred to me that as the incident had happened in my wife's marital bedroom, that would also have heightened her response.

I did not consider that Bernie staring obviously at my nakedness was an invasion of my privacy, after all I had not bothered to dress when I got up. But my wife considered Bernie's indiscreet stare to be an invasion of her martial privacy and fired a blast of disapproval at me in order to force me to act in a manner which she considered more proper, i.e. to cover my sexual bits.

This leads me back to the question of privacy. It seems to me that there is something about human relationships which requires us to live in groups and the closer these groups become the stronger the friendships are. But there are limits to how closely an individual can bond to other individuals without losing a sense of me-ness. There is a boundary within which we keep many of the thoughts of our inner self and we may not talk about them even to very close friends. At some level within myself, I was enjoying an unexpected opportunity to be an exhibitionist in front of both my wife and our friend. My reason tells me that one motive could have been to try and encourage favourable comments and positive reactions to the usually more hidden parts of my body from Bernie so as to draw the attention of my wife to what was available to her whenever she wanted it. But this is such a private thought that I am not sure if I should write it down. However, I suppose if I am to understand the complex interaction between friendship, approval and privacy I have to be honest with, and about, myself.

There is a continual tension between the need for privacy and the desire for approval. The need for approval brings us closer to our friends whilst the need for privacy pushes them away. The more private space you keep your friends out of, the less close friends you have. Privacy is not an attribute of an individual, as a solitary individual cannot be private, they can only be solitary. Privacy only has a meaning when an individual interacts with other people. It is a measure of the degree to which the individual allows the people they interact with to enter into their thoughts, their private physical space and to observe their intimate actions. If we can only be our true selves when we are naked then at some level we must let our close friends look on our nakedness.

The levels of interaction can be thought of as a sort of onion, with 'Me' at the centre. The next layer is close friends and family with whom you share mental and physical intimacies. Then there is a layer of professional and social contacts with whom you might share professional concepts and social interactions. Finally there is the rest of society who might approve or disapprove of the persona you choose to project to the world.

Within these broad circles you might also choose to vary the terms of your agreement with the members of any particular circle as to how much privacy you require and how much privacy you will allow them. These things are rarely discussed openly but can sometimes be inferred from the actions individuals take.

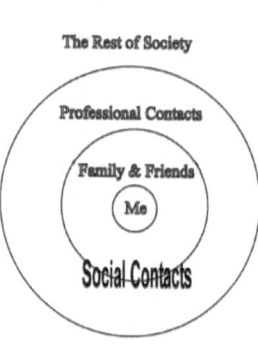

The Circles of Privacy

The theory of the etiquette of disregard offers an explanation of my wife's behaviour when she invited a woman friend into our bedroom whilst I was naked at the computer. My old college friend was not embarrassed about seeing me nude and being normally curious did not actively avoid taking 'an indiscreet glance' at my body. When my wife invited her into our bedroom I was concentrating on the computer and searching for the news item so I was not paying Bernie much attention but thinking back I recall that she stood next to me, to comment on the progress of the screen search. As she was standing close to my side while I sat at the computer it is certain that she would have been looking at me as well as at the computer. She would have no reason to follow the etiquette of disregard as she was there at my wife's invitation, I had neither objected or rushed to cover myself so as far as she was concerned that made my body a legitimate object of interest. Her curiosity must have been what made my wife uncomfortable so that she told me to put something on. Bernie and my wife both watched me as I bent down to pick up my pants from the bedroom floor and pulled them on. But once I had placed those few skimpy square inches of flimsy clinging cotton over my sexual organs my wife was happy to accept the encounter with our old college friend was now de-sexualized, even though I was worried that my underwear might be soiled and so make me an object of shame.

Making me aware of my own vulnerability, and the possibility of my intimate garments being held up to ridicule, was an implicit warning to me that I was not to take advantage of the situation to ogle Bernie's body, as she was not wearing much more than I was. After all the sage once said, 'People in glass houses should not take baths.' How right he was.

If we value the esteem of our friends then we must also trust them to see us as we really are when we live together. If we share our lives over a number of days then there are going to be times when we will drop the clothed mask we present to the outside world and reveal our true person. If we invite somebody into our inner circle of family and close friends then we must be prepared to trust them with our private selves and learn not to panic if we happen to see each other naked or, what is perhaps worse, revealed in our intimate undergarments. If we trust them we will not be embarrassed. But how does this trust, not to violate or ridicule personal privacy, develop in the more public context of a life drawing studio? As the novelist John Updike said of the life model. 'Nothing shields you from the artist's gaze except your bare skin.'

The beginning of this trust lies in the acceptance by everybody taking part in the life drawing class that what they are doing is absolutely normal. But to be a member of a group of ten or twelve fully dressed people forming a circle around a naked person who is sitting, standing or lying without moving a muscle and stare at them with a frighteningly intense gaze, to absorb every detail of their intimate appearance is not a normal event in the working life of a professor of mathematics.

Chapter 7 Ritual in the Nude

The distinction between what an individual exposes to public view and what they conceal or expose only to intimates is essential to permit creatures as complex as ourselves to interact without constant social breakdown. Each of our inner lives is such a jungle of thoughts, feelings, fantasies, and impulses that civilisation would be impossible if we expressed them all or if we could all read each other's minds. The formation of a civilised adult requires a learned capacity to limit expression of what is acceptable in the relevant public forum and the development of a distinct inner and private life that can be much more uninhibited, under the protection of the public surface.
– Thomas Nagel.

I was rapidly learning that there are fixed rules to the way a life studio is organised.

The life room is a sacred place. It is set aside from the normal teaching rooms, access to it during classes is tightly controlled, and has its own special cluttered presence.

Philosopher Alain de Botton pointed out that one of the ways all religions use to give their followers a sense of community is to create distinctive venues which express their beliefs and evoke enthusiasm for the notion of a special calling. He recommends that the venue should inspire visitors to suspend their customary self-centred attitudes in favour of immersing them in a different way of thinking. This social theory can be seen working in the life room. It is clearly a place for serious work. It is usually a large room with a raised stand, for the model to pose on, surrounded by a semicircle of benches or easels. We artists arrange our easels, benches or drawing boards around this raised stand so that we all have a clear view with sufficient distance to have a good perspective of the model. A space of about two metres is left around the model. This serves two purposes. It give the model a private space to display their nudity and it give the instructor room to stand in front of the students and point out features of interest to us. It also means all the artists are kept well away from the model.

The room is equipped with chairs, couches cushions and drapes for the model to use to support their body during long poses. This special space makes sure that the artists are unable to touch the model. The model, by shifting a pose, or leaning one way or another, can control what an artist sees. As I will discuss later in the chapter some models show remarkably little whilst others show a lot.

The model arrives and leaves wearing normal street clothing, undresses out of sight of the class and enters the circle of scrutiny in a robe. The nature of the pose is discussed with the instructor while suitable chairs, pillows, sheets and cushions are positioned to support the model's body in the desired position for a long pose, or the central area is cleared for a series of short 'gesture' poses.

Once the pose, or sequence of poses is agreed, the artists take up their chosen positions around the posing area and set up their drawing equipment. At its simplest this can be nothing more than pencil and sketch pad, at its most complex it can be a full set of oil paints, an easel, a canvas, a palette and a selection of brushes which needs a small suitcase to house them.

The model enters the room, demure and modest in robe and casual footwear, typically slippers, the pose is explained and tested. Whilst this is done the model remains robed but then there is a sudden transition. The model removes his/her footwear and robe to become naked for a few seconds whilst they move about and settle into the agreed pose. It is considered rude to stare whilst the model adjusts their body into pose. As they become still their nakedness becomes a uniform and the artists are now obliged to stare at every detail of the model's body. Not to pay attention means you are not taking the model's commitment to the pose seriously.

There is an unwritten contract of defined intimacy between the artist and model. Naked people have the power to shock us which is why as an artist I hide behind clothes but my model is driven out of all cover. I return to the unanswered question why do artist and model agree to take part in this unequal process?

It is a strange procedure by normal standards of behaviour. An adult woman, who I have never met before, comes into the room, takes off all her clothes and sits naked, just a few feet away from me. It is the stuff of teenage sexual fantasies, yet it is not erotic. If the woman was a patient, and I her doctor, then she would also allow me to touch her and move her body in order to examine it for the purposes of diagnosis. By an interactional process known as the etiquette of disregard, we would work through the abnormal situation and make the abnormal social circumstances seem as normal as we could. Something similar goes on the life room but it is not an etiquette of disregard which is at work because to disregard the detail of the model's nakedness would breach the unspoken contract. The basis of the contract is a shared but unarticulated interest in artistic endeavour. This is an interest most people can accept. Being an artist is a romantic and even admired calling. To practice the art of life drawing requires the discipline of observing the nude, hence the naked model has a higher aim than simple exhibitionism. They are providing the inspiration to create Art. By looking at their bodies and drawing what we see the artists keep their side of the bargain. But there is still an element of theatrical enjoyment in the model's motive. Winston had admitted to me that he enjoyed being nude in front of artists of the opposite sex. I was learning that art is essentially a sensual experience and modelling is part of the sensual practice of Art. As life model Kathleen Rooney said, 'I model because I can expose myself to strange, intelligent, fascinating people with virtually no risk whatsoever.'

Deborah had already explained to us that drawing should be spontaneous. She quoted the art critic Otto Benesch who said 'A drawing is an immediate emanation of personality, of the rhythm of life and its creative facility.'

But who's personality was being emanated? Mine or the model's?

Deborah had forced me to change my personality by driving me outside my comfort zone when she insisted I stare long and hard at Winston's willie until I could draw it accurately. Had I accosted Winston on the street, ripped of his pants and spent half an hour staring at his genitals I would have been arrested and locked up. But within the strangely skewed yet sacred space of the life class, I had been genteelly ridiculed for being too prudish to concentrate on Winston's most distinguishing male feature.

Within the life class all the normal rules of staring and intrusion of privacy are turned upside down. I was told I was insulting Winston by not looking closely at his genitals. Had I been sharing the changing room with him at a sports centre he would probably have punched me for staring at his groin. However, in the sacrosanct venue of the life class, amid the company of artists normality is different. You are told you must stare at the model's private parts and told off by the instructor and held in contempt by the model if you don't.

Deborah had insisted that I carefully observe and draw Winston's penis, but one week, when she was let down by a model at short notice, her words 'A model is not a sexual thing. It's simply a set of planes, curves and shadows you have to translate into lines on your paper,' came back to haunt her.

Rather than cancel the class Deborah found a model by asking one of her friends from the local playgroup to model for us. I recognised this press-ganged model as one of the young mums from the primary school where I served as a governor. I knew her as a friendly and out-going young woman whom I had spoken to, at the school bring and buy sale, only a week or so before. She recognised me.

'Hello Professor Cowley,' she said. 'I didn't know you were an artist.'

'Well I'm only learning to draw,' I said. 'So I'm not a real artist.'

'I'm going to model for you tonight,' she said. 'As a favour to Debbie.' She gave me a flirty smile, adding. 'I'm looking forwards to it.'

'I'll look forward to it too.' I said, wondering if it would be more embarrassing having to draw this young mum's genitals and mammary glands, than it had been to stare at Winston's crotch. She disappeared into the model's changing room while Deborah set up the stand and sorted the class out with boards and easels.

The young lady, whom I will call Pauline, soon appeared wearing a beach robe, from which her bare legs and arms projected. Deborah discussed a simple seated pose with her and she tested it without removing her robe.

'Are you ready?' Deborah asked.

Pauline smiled shyly, nodded and took off her robe. Beneath it she wore a brief bikini. Strangely enough Pauline, posing in beachwear, was much more of a sexual object than any of the nude models

I had drawn previously. I felt like I was drawing a pin-up and although Pauline tried hard to keep still, her slight shifts in position, made her seem far less comfortable than Eileen had been completely naked. Pauline seemed exposed even though she was wearing enough clothing to be completely decent on a public beach.

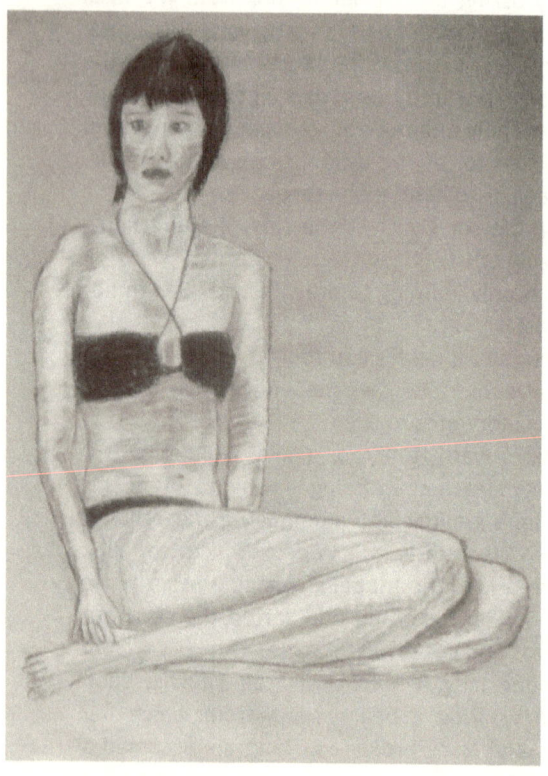

Sitting next to a women, effectively wearing just a skimpy bra and panties, and staring at her body, made me feel like a voyeur, rather than an impartial observer of a set of planes, curves and shadows. For the first time I understood how a nude model was less exposed than was Pauline in her bathing suit.

The bikini tantalised and drew attention to the sexual features of her body and kept reminding me I was drawing an attractive young woman. Pauline didn't help by watching me as I drew her.

I was not used to have having a model try to hold my gaze whilst in pose. Pauline kept catching my eye and smiling, as though she was seeking my approval. Of course, I smiled encouragingly back. But I had the expectation that a model is supposed to a passive object, not a person to interact with. I was concerned that I didn't know what this semi-naked woman wanted from me. I felt that as she deliberately caught my eye her exposed body became naked rather than nude. A nude is passive and is there to be observed, but a naked woman is a raw, revealed individual with her physical attractions and weaknesses blatantly on show. I did manage to draw Pauline, but the drawing has more the feel of playboy pose than a study in humanity. And looking at the drawing it appears stiff and closed.

The following week Deborah had to find another substitute to model at short notice. As the class was about to start she had called a friend who rushed round to help out. June was about the same age as Pauline but far less inhibited. She hadn't had time to collect a gown but it wasn't a problem for her. As the class was late starting and she had no robe to change into, she didn't bother with a changing room. She simply turned her back and undressed in front of the class. She didn't seem the least bothered to be seen undressing. Deborah said she was an artist and an experienced life model and thanked her for agreeing at a few minutes' notice to stand in for the booked model who hadn't turned up once again.

June was confident in her nudity, comfortable with her body, and did not seek reassurance or approval. Her poses were far more revealing than Pauline's had been the week before and she was much easier to draw. I could look at her crotch without her making me feel I was looking at something which was not supposed to be on public display.

She looked human, confident and completely self-assured. She was showing far more than Pauline had, but she was making less of a sexual exhibition of herself even though she had her legs apart and her genitals exposed.

By concealing the sexual features of her body, Pauline had drawn attention to them. By openly

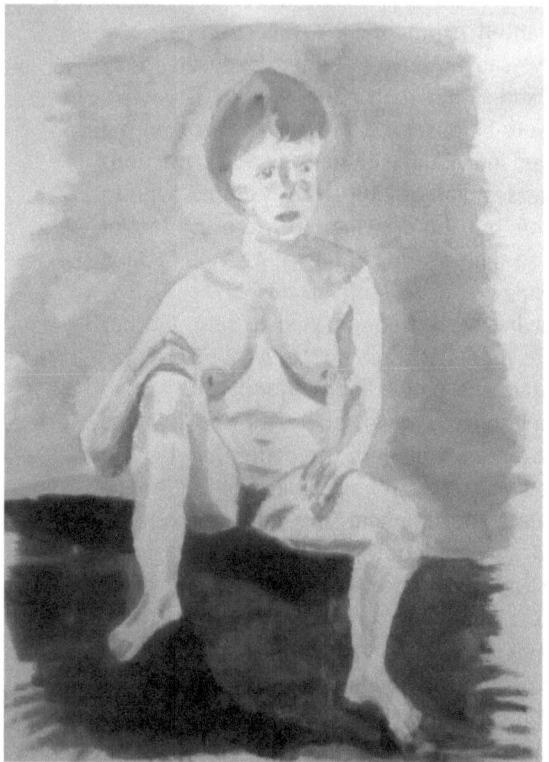

displaying them June made the point that she was simply a normal human being, without clothing. She knew she was an artist's muse, not a glamour pin-up.

Deborah asked June to start the session with a series of quick gesture poses and I did this drawing of her from the back.

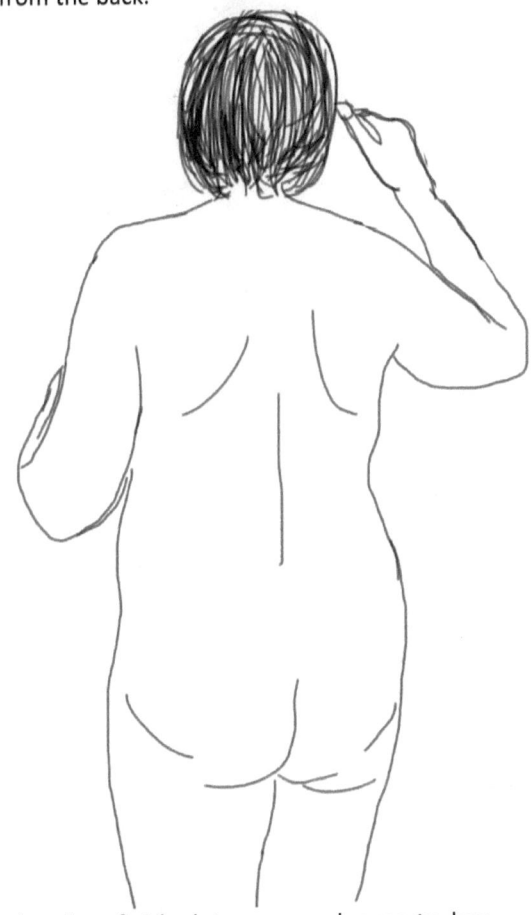

When the class finished June moved over to her clothes, which were neatly stacked on a chair in the corner of the room. As she had done at the start of the session she simply turned her back and put her clothes back on. First she pulled up her knickers and then put on her bra. I kept sketching as she put her clothes on and managed to capture a rapid gesture drawing of her as she dressed.

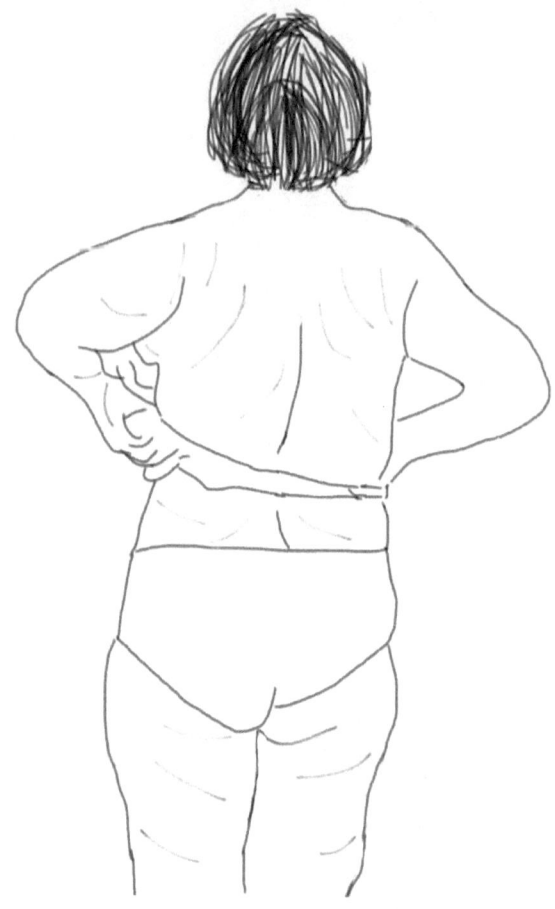

This quick sketch showing her, standing in her knickers, putting her bra on, is not a traditional life drawing. It is a voyeur's image of a naked woman dressing. She is not a model she is simply a woman putting her bra on, an unpretentious human act which is normally performed in private but as she did it in a drawing studio I could sketch it. This picture of June dressing is by far the most intimate of the drawings I did that evening. It is far more sexy than the nude view of her back and buttocks or the deliberately revealed swimsuit of Pauline, simply because it has a hint of the forbidden about it. It was captured in a matter of seconds, and was not a pose she intended to be drawn. She is adjusting her bra and she has not arranged her knickers modestly. I had accidently stumbled on the technique Degas used to draw his studies of women at their toilette. He posed them, but the effect was the same. A partly dressed woman who does not appear to be posing, but seems to be actually getting dressed or undressed, looks sexy to a male artist.

All clothes are different but all humans are basically the same. The only real differences are those due to gender and all adults know what both sexes look like naked. So when you draw a human's body you are reminded that you have more in common with other humans than you might think. Life drawing challenges me to accept that person on every level. That is why it evokes such a wonderful honesty. But I was still concerned about the subtle imbalance of power in a life-drawing classroom.

The following week, Deborah was once more without a model. This was when I found how delicate the balance of power between the clothed artist, the nude model and clothed instructor is. The students all turned up at the drawing class as usual. We were there with our drawing tackle, but Deborah kept looking at her watch with increasing signs of panic. No model appeared. Apparently the lady whom Deborah had booked hadn't turned up.

'What are we going to do?' Alice asked.

'Have you brought your robe?' I said. She just glared at me.

'I'll have to model for you,' said Deborah.

Wow, I thought. I'm going to get to see Deborah naked. This was going to be a teaching insight. I have occasionally dreamed that I was in the middle of delivering a lecture when I suddenly realized I had forgotten to dress and was standing naked in front of a few hundred undergraduates. I'm never quite sure if I manage to maintain lecture theatre discipline in my naked state, as I always fall though the floor into a deep sinkhole at that part of the dream and wake up before I hit the bottom.

How would Deborah run the class if she was nude and on the model's stand? The moment she moved and started to walk about instructing her class how to draw she would no longer be nude, she would be naked. I imagined her leaning over to guide the charcoal in my hand to illustrate how to capture a line in my drawing, as she so often did, but my immediate visualization featured her doing it without clothes. That would be really intimate one-to-one tutoring.

'Would it be better for one of us to model?' I said.

'No, you're all paid your fees for a life drawing class and as I have no model for you to draw I'll have to do it myself.' She said.

'How are you going to model and instruct?' I asked, wondering if she had a robe with her and if she would have to put it on to speak, as of course a model always remains silent when professionally nude.

'I'll have to tell you what to do before I start the pose and then have a look at how you've got on towards the end of the session,' she said.

'Great,' I said. 'Have you brought your robe?'

Deborah just looked at me. if I had been a small creeping creature I am quite sure that look would have instantly turned me into stone.

'Maurice,' she said. 'You will be drawing me clothed.'

'Oh,' I said, trying not to sound too disappointed and pervy. My hopes of seeing how she managed the delicate task of running a class whilst modeling nude had obviously been unlikely to happen. If she wanted to remain in charge of the class and keep her professional distance then it was clear that she could not take off the uniform of the wacky, creative art teacher and still remain the fount of all knowledge. For a teacher, distance is necessary to maintain a sense of mystery and superiority. The uniform of the role is a vital tool that she could not remove if she wanted to maintain her status with her students.

But even posing clothed, her body was sending out

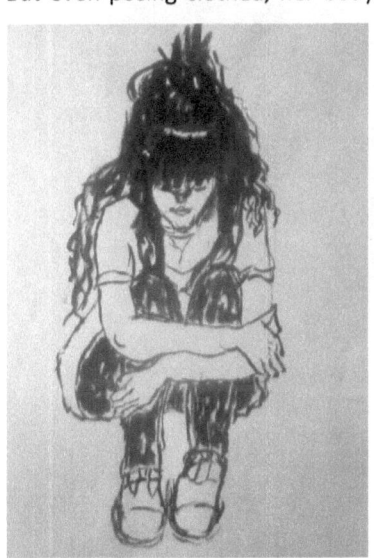

messages. The tightly closed posture she adopted for the first half of the session showed how annoyed she was at having to play the subservient role of model, whilst we, her students, were lording it in the authoritative roles of artists.

However, I noticed that the enforced stillness of posing seemed to sooth her spirit. After the debrief when she climbed back into the saddle of tutorship, commenting and advising us on how to improve our drawings, she was able to reassert her instructor status. Then, during the coffee break, she sounded off about unreliable models and got rid of the simmering thoughts that had festered within her as she sat in pose. Now she was able to take up a more open pose.

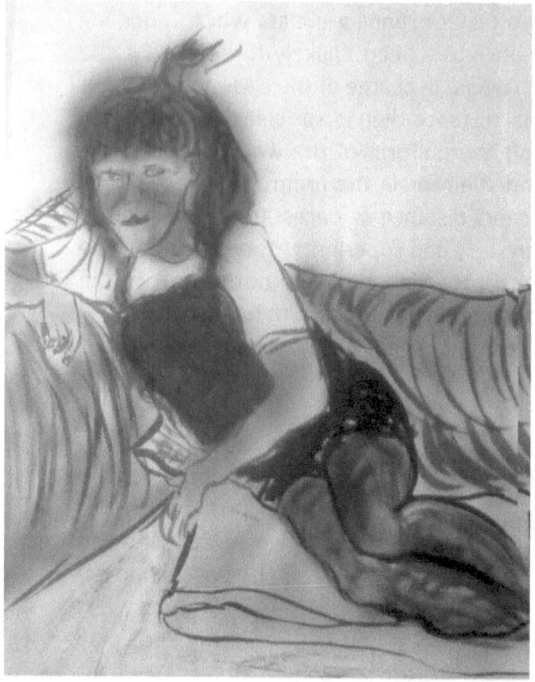

I thought she had a languidly sexy look on her face as I drew her. But staring up her skirt at her knicker covered crotch, in order to draw the join of her fully clothed legs, felt far more intrusive than drawing June's freely exposed pudenda. I imagined she must have been thinking about how I had assumed she would give up the protection of the teacher's uniform and show her body to the class, like a lowly hireling. 'Dream on Maurice,' I could feel her eyes saying to me. 'I'm still in charge'.

For Deborah to undress would have been a breach of the Life Room's rules that the artist and instructor must wear the uniform of his/her profession whilst the model must be clad in nudity as they jointly pursue the creation of Art. That is the contract both parties agree to. The model must accept the nude character when posing. Pauline posing in a sexy bikini was distracting because she was did not convey the Truth of Nakedness but used the erotic tool of skimpy dress to hint at something other than disinterested Art. She had not donned the nude uniform of the model and so did not fill the archetype's role of Muse in the Artistic Interaction. Likewise I felt intrusive whilst staring up Deborah's skirt, but was afraid to reject her as a model by not looking at what she had chosen to show me.

That evening as I made my way home I started to think more carefully about the power of uniforms and appropriate dress.

Chapter 8 Uniform Exposure

Ashamed of the many frailties they feel within, all men endeavour to hide themselves, their ugly nakedness, from each other, and wrapping up the true motives of their hearts in the specious cloak of sociableness, and their concern for the public good, they are in hopes of concealing their filthy appetites and the deformity of their desires.
Bernard Manderville philosopher, political economist and satirist

If you want to influence society you must wear the correct uniform and hide the body language of your naked self from hostile spectators. I keep reminding myself that Mark Twain pointed out that public nakedness is seen as a sign of weakness and a badge of unimportance. If Deborah had posed nude in front of her students we, and the college, might have judged her to be inappropriately undressed, no matter that as far artistic convention was concerned she would have been professionally nude. As it was, she remained within the acceptable dress code of the situation whilst posing, and retained her teacher's uniform to do so.

People do judge you by what you wear. Everybody must have experienced the dream of turning up at work and beginning to address a meeting before discovering you are completely naked. But to turn up at a formal black tie dinner in jeans and sweater is more far embarrassing than being seen naked by a house guest. (It the guest wasn't your friend you wouldn't have invited them to stay with you in the first place.)

The implication is that if you wish to be taken seriously then you must wear the correct uniform. If you are an academic you must wear a gown to graduation and casual jacket the rest of the time if you want to look professional. If you work in a laboratory you must wear a white coat with a row of pens in the pocket. If you want to convince your house guests you are an ageing hippy then must greet them naked in the early morning, on the corridors of your house.

People do change their view of you if they see you dressed in a way they do not expect. My wife has seen me naked for all of the 16 years we have spent in bed together. But no matter what I wear, or don't wear, she seems to be able to read my mind. I only seem to shock her if I wear a brand new shirt to clean the car. She judges the difference between nakedness and being respectable enough to engage in social intercourse with women friends, as a minimal covering of cloth over my genitals. In the instance I related previously, where she invited a friend into our bedroom while I was naked. I had to don a pocket handkerchief sized scrap of cotton fabric to meet her dress code for sharing social intercourse with another woman. Yet it was the collective view of the observers which created a dress code situation, not my indifference to clothing. I had no say in the matter. Once the visitor entered the room, my wife flipped my nudity into nakedness. Yet with to aid of just a tiny slip of white cotton, I became decent again.

Where the power to decide on the suitability of a particular dress code lies, is not a simple matter. Whether she would be judged to be appropriately dressed, acceptably nude, inappropriately attired, insufficiently covered or indecently naked was not something Deborah could predict with any degree of certainty when she decided what parts of her body she could reveal as she modelled. Dress codes are a function of the interaction between the *observed*, who chooses the clothes to wear or not wear, and the *spectators* who decide how they want to interact with the *observed*. Had Deborah chosen to pose nude, in place of the missing model, and a college administrator come into the classroom Deborah would have been considered indecently exposed in front of her students and dismissed from her tutorship. Even posing fully clothed she was inviting us all to pay much closer attention to her body than I would ever have dared to do under normal circumstances. Had I stared so intently up her skirt during the coffee break she might well have successfully accused me of sexual harassment.

An artist drawing a model is allowed to suspend all the usual social barriers about staring at someone else's body. The life room creates a zone of innocent freedom similar to that I described earlier when as a young academic, I holidayed with friends in a remote rural cottage.

My friends didn't really care what we wore or didn't wear, what we glimpsed of each other's bodies, or what we kept covered, as we shared holidays together. By choosing to live together in a small house we did not expect to maintain much privacy and we were able to be comfortably nude without being judged blatantly naked. We did not need the professional protection of a uniform to protect our true selves. The intimate nature of the holiday accommodation implied a mutual acceptance of the fact that we don't wear clothes all the time and we were not too uptight to admit it. While taking part in a life drawing session this freedom to look, without being intrusive, is not just permitted but enforced.

At college I never allowed my students to see me naked, even by accident, and so I could fully understand why Deborah felt she could not disrobe to pose for her students. It would have been unprofessional. But I suspect had she been at one of

107

our rural house parties she would have stripped off like everyone else, knowing she didn't need a uniform when on holiday.

Having gained some practise in drawing clothed figures I now found that if I was sketching my clothed friends I was applying the observational skills I had developed by drawing the most natural object in the world, the human body. Emboldened by being encouraged to stare at the join in Deborah's tights, I even plucked up the courage to sketch Alice, as she sat across from me, her artistically striped legs resting on the coffee table in a deliberately bohemian pose.

Seeing me drawing her she folded her arms and glared at me, but kept still while I finished the quick chalk and charcoal sketch.

'You've not made much of a job of drawing my face,' she said, looking at my attempt with a critical expression in her eyes. 'I look very grumpy.'

'I'm not used to drawing women with their clothes on,' I said. ' Your clothing is distracting as it masks your natural essence. Would you like to undress and I'll try and make you look happier.'

'My face was undressed,' she said.' 'and if you can't make my happy smiling face look better than that I don't want to even think about what you'll make the rest of me look like.'

'So you haven't actually said no,' I said. 'Shall I take that as a maybe and live in hope that one day you'll pose nude for me?'

Alice just gave me one of the stern school-ma'amly looks I had tried to capture in my sketch.

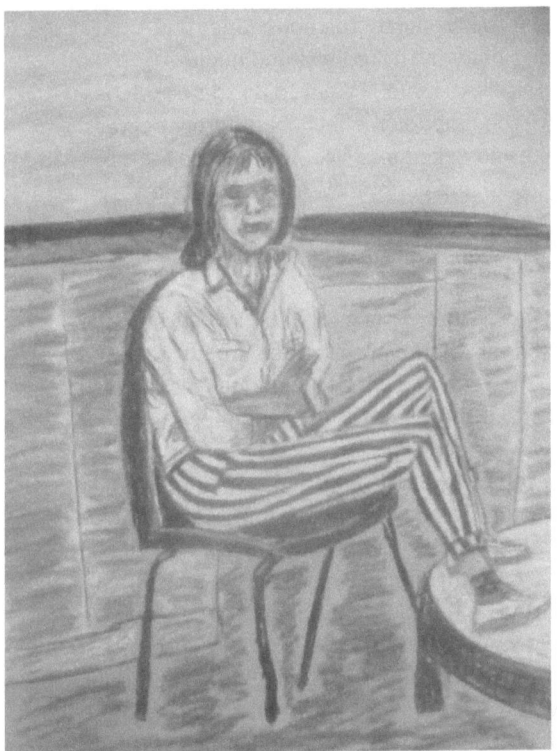

'If you want to draw a friend naked then ask Austin,' she said, pointing across the room to the only other man in our drawing group. 'You claim to have worked with him and he's a scientist too so suggest it to him as an experiment.'

Later in the pub I did just that.

Austin Sheerline lectured at my university and was a professor of chemistry, of about my age, who had also recently retired. He was attending the course for the same reason I was. He had been sent on the university pre-retirement course and been advised to take up drawing as a hobby. But Alice had given me a good idea. As he was a fellow scientist, I felt able to propose an experiment to him. It was an

109

experiment to investigate the boundaries and ambiguities between nakedness and nudity.

'Austy, old boy,' I said. 'I want to do some sketches to explore the emotional effects of different degrees of clothing and nakedness. Would you pose for me.'

He shrugged and grinned. 'Why not,' he said. 'We've played badminton together often enough for you to have seen what a marvellous physique I have.'

I explained that I wanted to investigate the implication of Mark Twain's idea about society's attitude to wearing clothes when he had written 'Clothes make the man. Naked people have little or no influence on society.'

'When you or I wear a suit or an academic gown,' I said to Austin, 'We know we are important and our clothes advertise just how important we are. Clearly we are at our most influential when we are formally dressed and at our least influential when we are naked. So how quickly do we lose influence as we discard items of clothing? I'd like to test this by asking you to first observe and then to comment on how it feels for me to draw you in various stages of undress? What area of coverage can you remove before you think you have lost all your influence? Is there a necessary minimum of clothing to maintain a facade of influence? And where is the statistical boundary of nakedness?

We decided to do a literature search about this question before carrying out the practical experiment, by looking for published photos of partly dressed politicians. This might give us some clues.

'Vladimir Putin.' Austin said, 'Did not lose influence by being photographed bare chested. He was seen as a strong out-door he-man, So I can safely discard my jacket and shirt without becoming unimportant. Even trousers are not vital. Silvio Berlusconi was frequently photographed in swimming shorts without being thrown out of office. It was only when he was revealed to have no national financial assets that he became uninfluential. So my trousers, shoes and socks can go as well. But when does acceptable clothing turn into virtual nakedness?'.

'Only sports shorts or swimwear seems to be an essential dress code in social circumstances.' I said. 'But is underwear acceptable? A pair of speedos may cover less than a pair of boxer shorts.'

'I'm sure if I stripped down to my underwear to attend the life drawing class,' I went on, 'Even if my motive was merely to reduce the imbalance of power between the naked model and the clothed artist, Deborah and Alice would be scandalized and I would be rusticated from the course. And I daren't even contemplate their response if I turned up in swimwear.'

'I've got a pair of black speedos I used to wear back in the sixties,' Austin said.

'Can you still get into them?' I asked.

'Certainly I can.'

'Well bring them along with your robe and I'll sketch you wearing them.' I said.

The following evening, while our wives were out playing bridge, he popped round to my place with his bathrobe and his speedos in a Lido bag. I welcomed him into the living room.

'I'd like to draw you with in key stages of dress and undress and then ask you how it felt while you were posing for me.' I said.

'In for a penny In for a pound,' he said. 'How do you want to start?'

'I'll let you undress and put your speedos on.' I said. 'I'll follow the rules of good practice recommended by our School of Medicine to all medical staff, and leave you alone to prepare yourself for this emotional examination.'

'Thanks, you're so considerate,' Austin said as I left the room for him to remove his clothes and squeeze into his speedos. When I came back he was standing in his trunks.

'I feel eighteen again, wearing these again,' he said. I didn't think he looked eighteen but I didn't comment.

'Just stand still.' I said. 'Are you comfortable being drawn like this?'

'Yes.' He said. 'No problem.'

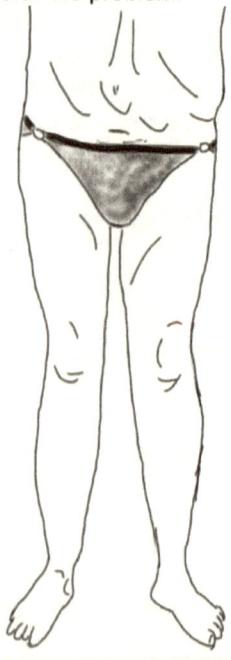

I finished the drawing and showed it to him. 'I didn't draw your face during this exercise,' I said, 'so you will remain ethically anonymous. How did you feel while I was drawing you?'

'Fine,' he said. 'But you've made me look a bit wrinkly.'

'You are a bit wrinkly,' I said. 'I'm only drawing what I see. Anyway let's try one of you in your underwear.'

'In my underwear,' Austin said, sounding a little uncertain.

'Yes, your boxer shorts will cover a lot more than that skimpy thing.' I said, 'I'll leave the room while you change.'

When I came back he was wearing close fitting white stretch boxer shorts and looking more nervous than I had expected, but he kept reasonably still while I drew him.

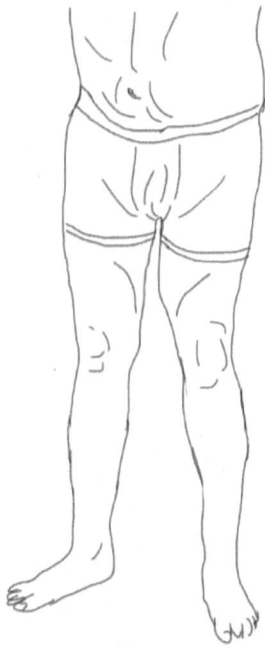

I showed him the sketch.

'You've drawn the outline of my penis,' he said.

'I could see the outline of your penis,' I said. 'Those shorts may cover more skin area than the speedos

113

but they cling more closely to your anatomy and show more topographical detail. How comfortable were you while I was drawing you.'

'A lot less than I when I had my trunks on.' He said. 'I felt dressed when I was wearing the trunks but I didn't in my underwear. I felt embarrassed when you were staring at my crotch, and kept wondering if my pants were stained. If I'd known you were going to draw me in my knickers I'd have worn loose fitting black ones.'

'So it wasn't the area of skin on show that you were bothered about? I bet you've wore those speedos many time in public.' I said.

'Oh yes,' He said. 'I cut a fine figure on the beach in my younger days and my girlfriends seemed to find speedos attractive and their cover sufficient to be respectable.'

'You've aged,' I said, avoiding adding any embellishment to keep the comment factual and neutral. 'Did you ever wear underwear on the beach?'

'Certainly not.' Austin said. 'I was far too shy to want causal friends to see me in public in my skimpies.'

'Obviously you were happy to wear skimpy things as long as you conformed to the uniform dress code.' I said. 'Speedos are swimwear, they are intended to be worn on a public beach. They cling but are reinforced around the genital area so they don't highlight your family jewels. Boxer shorts are designed to be worn under your trousers to protect your day clothes from staining. As long as you felt you were wearing the correct uniform then the area of skin covered didn't matter. I'll give you some privacy to take your boxers off. Will you put just your robe on and when I come back we'll measure both garments to see exactly how much cover each provided.'

I left the room while Austin removed his underpants and put on his robe. I came back with a ruler, to find him swathed in a bath robe and holding his boxers. I reached out to take them from him.

'I'll measure them myself,' he said. I didn't argue I simply reached down to the chair and picked up his speedos, unfolded my trusty wooden two-foot and measured them. He didn't object to me handling his trunks but letting me touch his boxers, still warm from his body, was obviously a step too far for him.

The surface area of the speedos was easy to calculate, they consisted of four equally sized right angle triangles with a base of 6.75 inches and height of 10 inches. Each triangle had a surface area of 33.75 square inches and the total of the four was 135 square inches. Austin checked and agree my calculation.

I had previously checked with the university's School of Medicine that the surface area of skin for a six foot tall man, average weight, man, such as Austin, was about 2800 square inches.

'You felt comfortably dressed in the speedos yet they covered only 4.8% of the surface area of your skin,' I said. 'You weren't bothered putting 95.2% of the surface of your body on public display. Now measure the boxer shorts.'

The surface area of the boxers was even easier to calculate as when laid flat they were formed of two equally sized and almost perfect rectangles. I handed Austin the trusty two-foot and he measured them to be 18 inches by 12 inches making a surface area of 432 square inches.

'That's interesting, ' I said. 'The boxers cover over three times the area that the speedos do, almost 16% of your skin, yet you were uncomfortable being observed in them. You said that you didn't like it when I stared at your underwear to draw it. And yet you had only 84% of your skin on display. It seems that the nature of the clothing matters more than the area it covers.' Austin nodded in agreement.

'Can we experiment further?' I said

'Yes,' Austin said, 'This is interesting. I hadn't realised how sensitive I was to the agreed purpose of the clothing I wear.'

'That's the power of the right uniform.' I said. 'Now I want to draw you in your robe.'

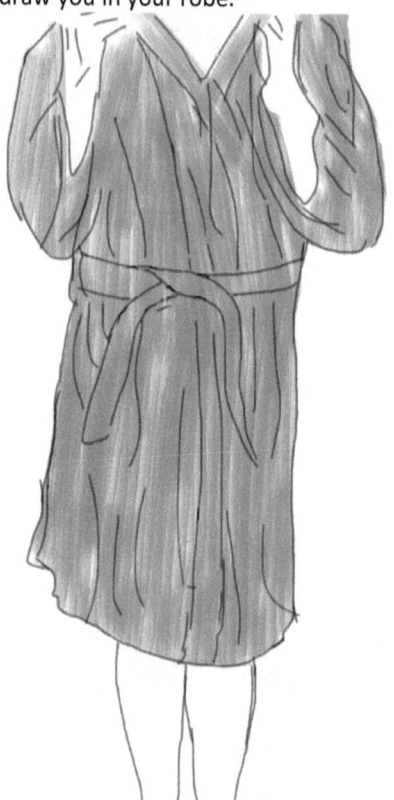

Austin stood up and held the lapels of his robe, like a Victorian gentleman in a smoking jacket.

I finished the drawing, which being quite complex, took some time then I showed it to him. 'How comfortable were you while I was drawing you this time?' I said.

'Totally,' he replied.

'But would you be happy to give a lecture to a class of first year undergrads dressed only in this robe?'

'I'm quite sure I wouldn't. as they would think I had overslept, or had seriously sartorially challenged taste, if I stood in front of them like this.' He said.

'But you're perfectly decent,' I said. 'You're only showing your lower legs, arms and head.'

'As long as I stand still,' he said with a grin. 'But I move about in a vigorous manner when I'm lecturing, on the premise a moving target it harder to hit. And who knows what revelatory shocks I might deliver to my impressionable young audience if I happened to twirl my skirts too high.'

'Let's try something else.' I said.

'What? ' he asked.

'Kick off your slippers, drop your robe completely, face me and stand still while I do a nude torso study.'

'Are you sure I won't be recognisable in your sketch?' He said.

'I'm only going to draw your torso and lower limbs,' I said. 'Not your face.'

'Do you know the story of the Parson's Pleasure bathing site they once had at another place?' I said. 'And story of my famous part namesake Professor Sir Maurice Bowra?'

'No.'

'I'll tell you the story before I draw you,' I said.

There's a section of the River Cherwell that runs through the university parks and for many years it allowed nude bathing for university men.

To avoid inappropriate exposure there was a footpath round the area with a high fence. Punting ladies were advised to disembark and walk passed the site behind the fence so that they would not be offended by the sight of the naked dons or their equally naked students. This site was closed in 1991 and the fence dismantled, so the tradition of nude frolics, which Hugh Trevor-Roper, Isaiah Berlin, C.S. Lewis and John Sparrow had all enjoyed, along with my namesake Maurice, came to an end. I heard Lewis once tell of a time in the 1930s when all these worthy gentlemen were sunning themselves *en natural* when a group of female students drifted passed and stared and shouted at the naked gentlemen. All except Maurice rushed for towels to cover their male bits, he covered his face with a handkerchief and placidly continued to soak up the sun, oblivious to the laughter and lewd shouts of the young women. Afterwards when Lewis asked him why he had covered his face and left his genitals on display he said. 'I don't know about you Clive, but in Oxford I am better known to the women students by my face'.

Reassured Austin dropped his robe. Folded it carefully, placed it on a chair and turned to face me.

'And I would have thought most people know you better by your phiszog rather than your phenis.' I said looking pointedly at Austin's sex.

''Unfortunately you are correct.' Austin said. 'But if your wife comes in while I am standing here like this that situation may change.'

'But she's encouraged me to get out, find a hobby and do something with my time.'

'But Maurice, you have not got out. You have persuaded me to stand naked in the middle of your living room. And as your wife will be back soon I'm beginning to wonder if it was wise to humour you.'

'Well, Austin, let's get on with it. Stand up straight and keep still please.'

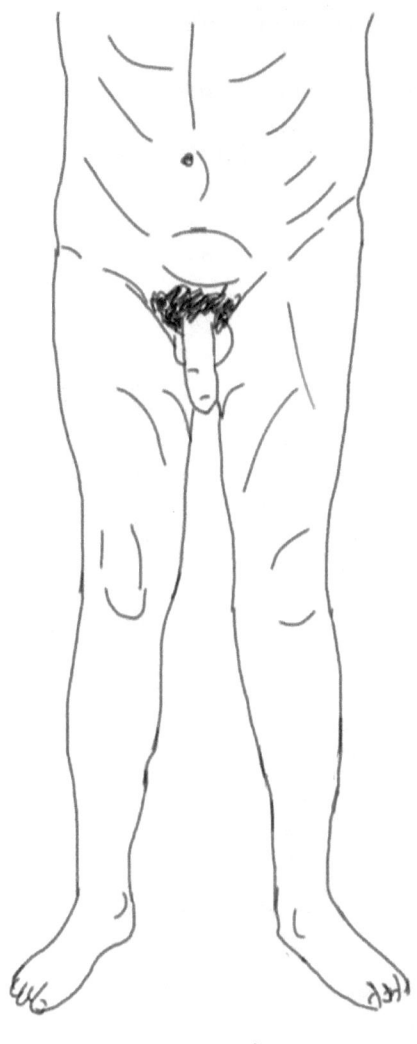

I drew his torso and legs.

'Please put your robe and slippers back on and I'll show you my drawing,' I said.

He did and then looked at the sketch.

'You've made me look even more wrinkly without my pants,' he said.

'You are more wrinkly without your pants.' I said. 'I keep telling you that I only draw what I see.'

'Well at least I stayed relaxed and wrinkly.' Austin said with grin.

'Let's try one more test,' I said. 'Please open your robe, slip your right arm out of it and let it hang from your left shoulder. '

He let his robe fall open and away from his right side, revealing his genitals.

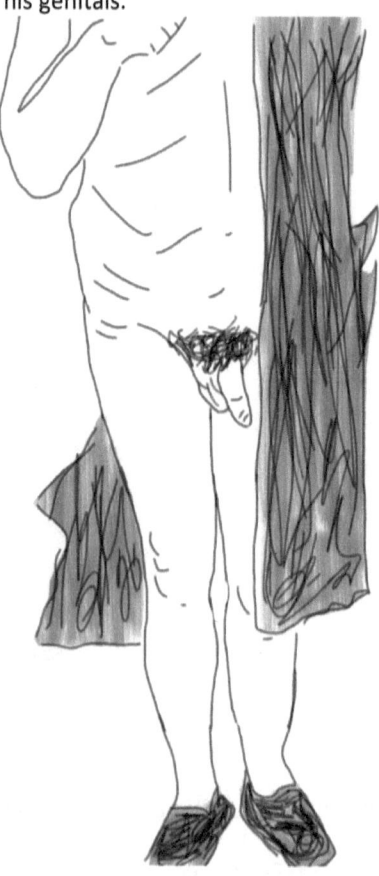

120

He did as he was told and then stood completely still while I drew him. I was careful not to catch his eye and to keep my gaze lowered so he could not see my expression.

Once I had finished the drawing I asked him to close his robe and tell me how it had felt to be drawn with it hanging open.

'Very uncomfortable.' He said. 'I felt far more vulnerable and exposed, than I had when I was completely nude, even though I had the robe over my shoulder.'

He went to describe how he felt as I drew him.

'I was aware that my pecker was hanging out for another man to stare at. Even though I know you are an old friend and colleague and I was a willing model I still felt intruded upon. I met myself be put into a naked and inferior position and then I had to watch you, while you were eyeing up my nakedness to see how best to draw my manhood and wouldn't look me in the eye. That was un-nerving. I had approached this simply as a detached experiment. I had decided to act as your model in the interests of science and developing a better understanding for myself. But when I stood with my robe half open and groin exposed I felt I had no physical secrets. You were dressed and human, and I was a half-naked animal. When I occasionally caught your eye I thought I saw a fleeting expression of scorn, it felt like you quickly controlled the look as you started to sketch me'.

'Did you feel scorn?' he asked. 'Or was it my imagination.'

'No, I didn't feel any emotion about your sex organs.' I said, 'I was just concentrating on how to draw you accurately and having to draw the robe as well as your body, made it more difficult. To be honest I was using your cock as a landmark to fix the line of your robe which is why I kept staring at it.'

'I felt as if you were looking at me as though I was an object,' he said. 'And I felt different because of the prurient attention you seemed to be paying to my genitals.'

'But you weren't technically naked,' I said. 'You still had your robe over your shoulder and your slippers on your feet. In fact you had far less skin on display than when you wore the speedos. You were 50% covered.'

'That only made it worse,' he said. 'Having slippers on and a robe over my shoulder, yet with my cock hanging out on display made me feel more than naked. You spent ages staring at my penis. And all I could see in your face was the smug look of a secure, confident and fully dressed man staring at my cock and judging it. My genitals were completely and irrevocably exposed and I kept seeing the self-satisfied look on your face and I felt that must have shrivelled with my exposure to cool air. You staring at my limp phallus made me feel like a powerless victim. All my normal props of professorial power had disappeared with my clothing, and it made me feel extremely uncomfortable.'

'So it's not the absolute area of skin you expose, it's whether the uniform you wear is appropriate.' I said. 'You were comfortable as a nude model and wearing swimwear as these are acceptable uniforms to be seen in but you were uncomfortable in your underwear and with your robe falling open to show your normally private parts. It seems that context is everything.'

All normal human beings have a concept of who they are. This concept of 'me' is usually predicated on the idea that 'I am basically a good person' and forms the basis our idea of our own self-worth and social value. But there are parts of our inner life where we have instincts and urges which we are not always willing to share even with our closest family or friends. There are some thoughts which we always want to keep private, even though all humans have similar instincts. We have an idea of ourselves which is positioned within a social space whose boundaries are fixed by the requirements of the society we live in, by the professional roles we carry out and by the approval or disapproval of our family and friends. If we transgress these boundaries then our status within the hierarchy of our social network falls but if we meet the expectations of those whose opinion we care about then our status raises. This means that our social status is a continually fluctuating quantity which increases when we receive approval and falls when we receive disapproval. The value of our social status within any of our groups or social networks is continually being negotiated by our actions and the judgement those actions cause to occur within the minds of those we interact with. Thus we interpret our status by the words, and body language, which signal to us the thoughts the 'inner selves' of the people in our group.

There is a pecking order which arises from the hierarchy of the social network which confers on some individuals the power to judge and puts other individuals in the position of being judged. When Austin was nude or wearing skimpy swimwear, an etiquette of disregard seemed to limit his unease when non-sexual nudity or near nudity was involved. But when he was exposed by improper dress he was embarrassed.

However, in modern society there is no single, overarching moral framework of reference which an individual can use to make absolute decisions about the appropriateness of dress in an fundamental sense. Each privacy group we belong to (and by privacy group I mean the individuals who we allow to share our more intimate thoughts and personal actions without embarrassment) has its own rules by which approval and disapproval is mediated. As my Revd friend remarked after he met me naked on the corridor in the early morning outside the bathroom, whilst wearing only M&S shorts himself, he did not disapprove of my lack of dress. Had he been wearing a suit and had I met him in the street he would have been surprised and disapproving if I had chosen to be naked. My physical state would have been identical in both instances but his response would have been different so it is not just a question of who sees your naked body, but also the context in which they see it. This naturally led me into thinking about the question of appropriateness and the audience who are empowered to judge such appropriateness.

It would have been inappropriate for Deborah to pose naked whilst in the role of instructor of the life drawing group and Austin also found it inappropriate to pose with his robe open, but he was quite happy to stand nude and be drawn. The strange protocol of sharing our naked bodies with other humans is extremely complex. However, soon after this little experiment in exploring the limits of undress, I found that I was suddenly thrust into a set of circumstances which allowed me to observe how this worked in more serious circumstances.

Chapter 9 Testing the Etiquette of Disregard

When someone nude comes into view, there is a desire to avert one's eyes, to look the other way, or if one is required to look, to look minimally and to not really see, to be casual about it, to disregard the shock of nudity. For nudity, for most people is psychologically blinding because we have all been trained in the etiquette of disregard, which requires us not to stare when the person we would stare at might be embarrassed.
- Lois Shawver

During a discussion I once had about appropriate dress and undress with my friend, the Revd Jowett, he had said 'I expect someone in a position of life or death over my body [i.e. his doctor] to be manicured, smooth, polished and unruffled. Nothing else quite cuts the mustard.'

What he hadn't mentioned was how he would feel if his doctor was an attractive professional woman and he had a critical reason to expose his naked body to her professional scrutiny whilst under the watchful gaze of her attendant female nurse? I was about to find out.

I will explain the circumstances. I developed a small growth on my left arm. A surgeon friend of mine, from our university hospital, noticed it and advised me to have to it removed by Dr Mercedes Bens, a mutual colleague who he assured me was the best in her field. I showed the lesion to my GP who duly referred me to Dr Bens at my own university hospital. She turned out to be a charming and attractive lady in her mid-forties. I took to her immediately, we shared some gossip about the university before she examined the offending lump. She held my arm and examined my skin and I found

125

her touch gentle and caring. She advised the removal of the growth and in due course she cut it out, fortunately it turned out to be only pre-cancerous. When I returned a month after the removal of the lesion, she told me the scar was healing well.

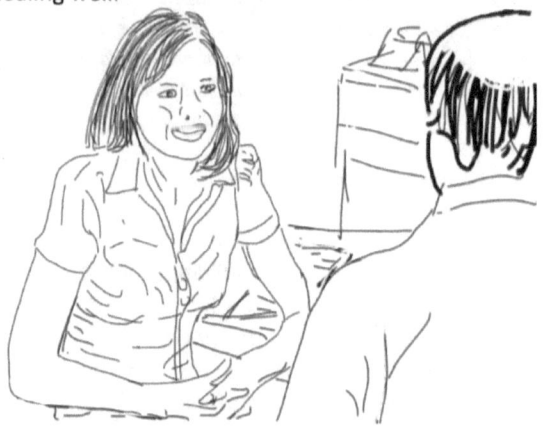

She made an appointment to see me six months later and advised me to inspect all my skin regularly, using a full length mirror, and watch out for any new outbreaks or changes in existing moles etc. This I did and noticed areas which I had not been aware of before. I noticed four slight changes in my skin. The first was small mole just below my left shoulder blade, the second another small mole on my left buttock, the third a small outcrop of flesh growing on my right thigh just below my testicles and finally a small dark mole which appeared below my belly button just in the upper limit my pubic hair. When I considered the impending follow up appointment I realized that I would have to undress for her to inspect these new blemishes on my skin.

I arrived in good time for our appointment, only to be told that the doctor was running late and so I sat in the waiting area reading the daily papers on my ipad. I was wearing a shirt and tie with a tweed sports jacket over grey formal trousers and looked the part of the respectable academic. Although I was nervous, as I knew I would soon be required to undress for this charming lady doctor to inspect the suspect blemishes, I tried not to show it. I argued to myself that this was an opportunity to observe how she, and her nurse responded to my exposure, and how I felt about the experience.

The doctor was running forty-five minutes late so I sat for an hour worrying about what was about to happen. The nurse who assisted Dr Mercedes was calling earlier patients through. The patients were mainly teenage girls and their mothers. I was the only male patient waiting and I kept smiling at Dr Mercedes's nurse, playing the role of the benign emeritus academic to the full and letting my shirt and tie give me gravitas. The nurse was in her late twenties with blonde hair swept back tightly into a bun. She looked harassed and tired.

Finally she called my name. 'Professor Cowley will you come through please.'

She took me into a small waiting room with a metal trolley, a table and a chair.

'Dr Mercedes won't be long', she said.

'I've been quite happy reading the papers until she is free,' I said, smiling at her. She smiled back. I was really working at being charming so as to engage with her as a real individual, not just another passing patient. I was doing friendly rather than cold and professional. She went into the next room closing the door after her. I decided to remove my jacket and put it on the back of the chair. I undo my left sleeve cuff ready to show the site of the previous operation. I carried on reading The Times on my ipad. I expected the consultation to take place in this side room and was mentally preparing myself to remove my clothing.

127

The door opened again and I looked up, expecting Dr Mercedes, to walk through but it was the nurse. I smiled at her and she smiled back. She was treating me like a real person so my charm offensive seemed to be working.

'Dr Mercedes has a student with her today, would you mind if he takes part in the consultation?'

This was a surprise. I was going to have a young man watching me get naked too. Being a student the young man might not yet be skilled in the etiquette of disregard. I gave a mental shrug, thinking it would be interesting to compare his behaviour with that of the consultant and her nurse. There was also a source of potential embarrassment for the student who would have a pretty blonde nurse watching him while he handled the intimate skin of an older naked man who was an emeritus professor of the university which ran his hospital. So no pressure.

'I don't mind at all, he's welcome to join in.' I said. The nurse thanked me and disappeared once more. A few minutes later she called me through. Dr Mercedes was sat at a desk and smiled at me as she invited me to sit down. I was carrying my jacket and ipad, was still wearing my tie and had my left sleeve cuff undone. I placed my jacket on the back of the chair and put the ipad down on her desk.

'How are you doing?' she asked. She is a petite lady with a trim figure and large eyes, and was wearing black trousers and yellow blouse with an open neck and short sleeves.

'I'm fine,' I said, 'you did a good job. It's healed well.'

'I'm sorry you've been kept waiting so long,' she said.

'It wasn't a problem,' I said smiling at her. 'I have the Times on my ipad to amuse me, and you must be busy to be running so late.'

'It has been busy,' she said and her face lit up in broad smile.

For a minute or two we discussed the merits of downloading newspapers and she told me that she had bought herself an ipad and she loved it although she wasn't a technical person. She was charming and showed interest in me as an individual, agreeing it was useful to get the daily paper downloaded to read before she set off for work. While we were chatting, the nurse stood quietly by the door and the student stood at the far end of the room taking no part in this chit chat between university colleagues.

Dr Mercedes asked me to roll up my left sleeve and show her the scar. I did so and she looked at it and ran her finger over it, very gently. She called the student over to look at it. Then she asked if I had been following her advice to check myself carefully and if I had any concerns. I took a deep breath to stifle the squadrons of butterflies I could feel swarming in my stomach as I began to explain.

'Yes.' I said. 'Since having that scare I've been inspecting my skin more carefully. I don't really trust it to behave.' Dr Mercedes smiled. 'I've noticed four areas with unusual growths.'

'Have they appeared recently or is it that you've just noticed them?'

'Three of them are recent and the other might to have been there for a while but it's stable.'

'Where are they?' she asked.

'One's on my back under my right shoulder blade,' I said. 'One's on my right thigh,' I pointed to the area at the top of my leg. 'One is on my left buttock and the other is here on the lower part of my stomach,' I said indicating the area just above my genitals. 'Would you mind looking at them and telling me if I've anything to worry about?'

She looked me up and down and smiled a warm smile. 'I told you to check yourself, Professor

Cowley. Of course I'll need to examine you.' She stood up. 'Follow me.'

She led me though an adjoining door into another examination room. There was a blue leather examination couch with a large roll of paper to cover it and a chair. A modesty curtain hung from the ceiling but it was pushed against the wall and would remain there for the whole of the examination.

'Undress and I'll be right back,' she said spreading a fresh paper cover on the couch. As she left the room she said in a stage whisper to the nurse, which I was obviously intended to hear. 'Slip his ipad into the drawer while he's not watching.' She closed the door leaving the decision of how far to undress up to me.

I now had to remove my clothes and allow her to handle my skin in four distinct and agreed regions of increasing intimacy.

She had told me to remove my clothes in private so that I would not be embarrassed by being watched as I revealed my body. Now I really understood the wisdom of the professional advice I had applied when drawing Austin. This procedure clearly separates the act of undressing from the state of-nakedness. It also helped me understand why most models prefer to undress in private and then remove their robe quickly to minimise voyeurism during the removal of intimate items of apparel.

Dr Mercedes had left the decision of how far I stripped down to me. She hadn't given me any precise instructions on how much I clothing I should remove, and I did wonder if I should get undressed completely. I decided to shed everything but my underwear and socks. I would remove my academic uniform completely and leave the option of further divestment for Dr Mercedes to instigate at the appropriate moment when she was ready to inspect the more sensitively situated sites.

I was curious about the etiquette she would use during the process. I wondered whether I should lie on the couch and act the role of patient. I decided it would be better for the experiment to sit on the side of the couch so that I could stand up to meet her and show her the mole near my shoulder whilst standing next to her. This would allow me to be an active co-operator in the examination.

A few seconds later she came back into the room followed by the male student and the nurse. I smiled at her and she smiled back, looking me straight in the eyes. The student looked at the floor and the nurse looked at me and whilst careful to avoid eye contract quite obviously inspected my body. This was understandable as there is nothing quite so ridiculous as an almost naked man in skimpies and socks. The briefs covered my sexual organs but showed their general shape. I stood up to meet Dr Mercedes as she entered the room and stepped towards her. My genitals were covered so I didn't feel naked and I knew my pants were clean. The briefs were not much different in covering power than Austin's speedos had been. Dr Mercedes held my gaze for a moment and then deliberately inspected my body as she spoke.

'Good,' she said. I would have been far less comfortable and confident without the underpants. 'Where's the first one?'

'Here,' I said turning my back towards her and reaching round with my left hand to point to my right shoulder blade. I could feel the warmth of her body as she stood close to me quickly followed by the soft touch of her fingertips as she inspected it. She was not wearing gloves.

'That's fine,' she said. 'And the next?'

'The rest are hidden by my underpants,' I said. 'Should I remove them?'

'You can just push them well down.' She said. 'You don't have to take them off.'

I stood by the couch and pushed my underpants down to my knees, spread my legs apart, pulled my testicles to the side with my left hand and pointed to the small growth at the top of my inner right thigh with my right. She leaned over and looked closely at my upper thigh while I held my genitals aside for her to get a good view of the top of my leg. My hand effectively shielded my penis and testicles from the student who still seemed to be concentrating on his shoes and the nurse who was looking in my direction with her gaze positioned well below my eye level. I did occur to me that if I had been wearing a swimming costume on a beach I would never have dreamt of deliberately handling my testicles whilst two women were watching me, let alone pulling my trunks down to give them a better view. The rules of appropriate behaviour are so different when you undress for a doctor or nurse. You are allowed to touch yourself in ways which would be considered indecent if done in public.

'It's a simple skin papilloma, nothing to worry about.' Dr Mercedes said and smiled encouragingly at me. 'Now lie back on the couch, and let me examine the other delicate one.' She straightened up and stood to the side to give me room to swing my legs onto the couch.

I lifted my legs and lay back on the couch. The nurse was still looking at my body and would not make eye contact at all, the student still seemed to be mainly looking down and just shooting quick glances at me. I'm used to being naked in bed and in the mornings as I go to shower, but there were two women and a young man who I did not know in the room and I was showing them my most intimate parts. My genitals, lower belly and pubic hair were all on display.

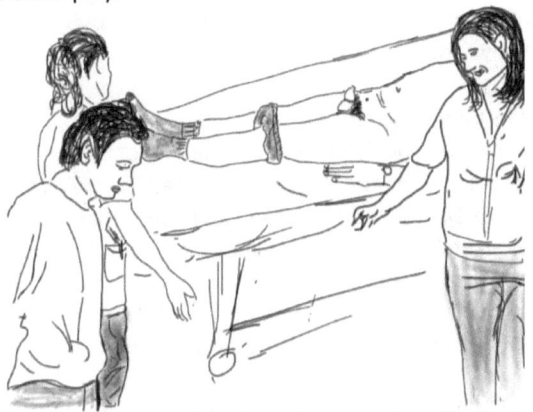

I was lying on an examination couch, effectively naked in a room of fully dressed people. Only my knees were partly covered by my briefs and I wasn't going to be able to pull them up until Dr Mercedes told me to. Now I was uncovered I felt more comfortable about it than I had felt just before I pushed my pants down. Nobody had screamed, nobody had ran away and nobody had criticised me for exposing my genitals. Once I was naked it was done and I wasn't suddenly going to become more naked.

My bare body was the centre of attention for an audience consisting of a charming and attractive consultant dermatologist in her mid forties, a pretty blonde nurse in her late twenties and a young male medical student who looked about nineteen. I could feel their eyes staring at my sex and I felt vulnerable. Why I am doing this? I thought. Then I reminded myself I needed the blemishes examined and was still interested in observing how personal relationships changed when I removed my academic uniform and allowed strangers to see me naked. My discomfort was simply an interesting consequence.

The medical staff were certainly looking at everything I normally kept private. I wasn't sure if they were judging me or simply observing me professionally and impersonally. Then it did get more personal.

The other two watched closely as Dr Mercedes gently touched my pubis to feel the nature of the blemish. The student and the nurse stared at my naked groin as Dr Mercedes leaned closer and using both hands stretched the skin just above my penis to look at the effect on the swelling.

'Come here Thomas,' Dr Mercedes said to the student who was standing well back. ' Look closely at this lesion. It's hard, dark and slightly crusty and if you look closely to you can see small white spots in the centre.' while she was talking she was manipulating my skin to display the various features of the lesion as she described them to the student. Her hand was less than an inch from my penis as she gently handled me. Then she stepped back, turned her head out of the line of sight of the nurse and the student, and smiled at me. It was a reassuring smile and was followed by a wink. This wink felt like a conspiratorial warning to a fellow teacher not to worry what the student might say as the mole wasn't dangerous. I kept my face straight and my body still.

'What is it?' she said to the student. 'Can you diagnose it? Is it serious?' The student was now peering down at my exposed groin. 'You'll have to feel it,' she told him.

Dr Mercedes, was using bare hands and her touch was warm and gentle. The student was wearing thin rubber gloves as he reached out to investigate the mole and they felt cold and clinical. He kept well away from my penis, but still seemed uneasy at handling the skin so close to my sex organs. His touch was much less assured and gentle than Dr

Mercedes's. Perhaps he was nervous about fiddling around close to the genitals of someone who moments before had looked and behaved like one of his professors and whom he knew was some sort of doctor, even if he didn't know I was a doctor of mathematics.

Dr Mercedes had decided I was a good visual and tactile aid for the study of benign skin growths. Of my own free will and accord I had given permission to be touched, looked at and examined. I had volunteered to undress for her and her student. I had not been pressured to place myself in this exposed state and so she felt free to use my naked body as a training aid. Her tone of voice as she instructed the student was calm and professional. But for the young trainee doctor it must have been difficult to handle the exposed body of a man he had met as a senior professional of the university just minutes before. And he was having to handle me in front of the nurse, who was watching him, and what he was doing to me, intently.

'You have to palpitate it to feel its structure.' Dr Mercedes ordered him, seeing he was hesitant about touching me too freely. He did as he was told and prodded my groin so vigorously I could feel my penis roll about. He pretended not to notice as he stretched the skin around the mole. He stepped back and Dr Mercedes stood by my side, pointing down at my chest.

'This man has fair freckly skin,' she told him, and ran the tip of her finger lightly over the small areas of discoloured skin on the right hand side of my naked chest. Her touch was as light as the touch of a butterfly's wing brushing my skin. 'And I've treated him for Bowen's disease on this arm.' she reached over and touched the scar on my left arm which lay by my side.

She had already inspected all my growths and I was thinking to myself, that I would soon get dressed. But Dr Mercedes had different ideas.

She turned slightly sideways, and leaned over me and circled the mole slowly and deliberately with the tip of her a finger.

'How wide a peripheral area of skin should you inspect?' she asked Thomas. Her touch was as gentle as a sensual lover as she stood stroking my pubis. I started to worry that I might become erect. She continued to circle the mole with her finger to focus her student's attention on the extent of area of skin she wanted him to diagnose. She was giving a simple training demonstration, but she was encouraging the student and the nurse to look directly at me. I didn't want to get an erection, so I concentrated on watching the student, who was certainly not going to make eye contact or encourage me to get excited. It worked. I managed to suppress the urge to arousal.

'What do you think it is?' Dr Mercedes asked.

'Serorrhoeic Keratoses?' the student replied.

'Quite right' she said. And then she stood between me and the others, looked down into my eyes and smiled. 'It's nothing serious, just a benign build-up of ordinary skin cells. Nothing to worry about.' Her grin was infectious as she patted the keratoses and my pubic hair. Her touch felt like an electric tingle and I couldn't stop myself beginning to twitch. This was not something I had thought would happen. I had not expected to become aroused during the examination and I began to panic that any attempt on my part to hide an erection with my hands or cover it with my underpants would not be appropriate behaviour in front of the young man. Then Dr Mercedes upped the embarrassment factor as she nudged me with her hip and said.

'Can I have you the other way up please?' she said, adding, 'To look more closely at the other two lesions.'

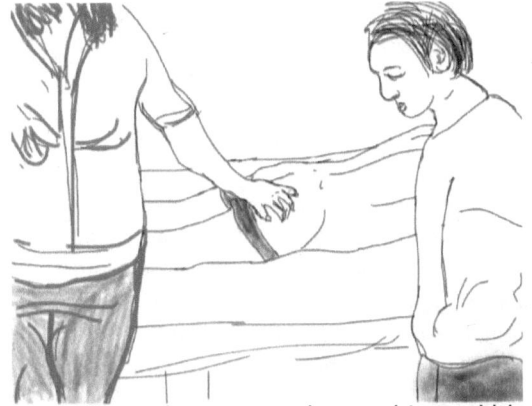

I was going to have to stand up and it would be obvious I was too aroused to hang vertically. I wasn't sure how far above the horizontal I might be but I didn't seem to have any choice. I had volunteered and now I was about to find just if the etiquette of disregard was really any protection again humiliation. Better get it over with, I thought, with as much good grace as possible. After all I had set out to study the limits of nakedness and now I was exploring its outer boundaries.

'Certainly' I said. 'If that's what you want.' Dr Mercedes, looked down and smiled, before positioning herself between me and our audience. She shielded my partial erection from their view while I stood up. I could feel my face getting warm, and I don't usually blush, but I did then. To ease the tension I glanced down and said. 'Excuse me.'

Dr Mercedes had a twinkle in her eye as she said. 'I need to be able to examine both lesions,' she said. 'So don't pull your pants up *at the back*.'

I took that as an instruction to cover my penis while she stood between me, the nurse and student, effectively obscuring what was happening in my sexual region. As unobtrusively as I could I adjusted my briefs to cover myself even though the tenting effect was obvious. I arranged the rear of my briefs so that I was showing my buttocks and lay face down on the couch as I had been told to. My erection hadn't gone down, in fact it had got firmer as Dr Mercedes had acknowledged it with what I can only describe as an 'old fashioned look'. But at least it was now safely out of sight, inside my underpants and beneath my body. I folded my arms under my chin and lay still. I had not expected to get aroused during the examination so it was not a scenario I had mentally rehearsed. I had no plan to follow. I felt a fluttering in my stomach because I knew that Dr Mercedes was aware of my condition but I felt reassured that she had positioned herself to hide my erection from the others to spare me greater embarrassment.

'Thomas,' she said. 'What is that?' I half expected him to say 'Dr Cowley's bum' but then I felt a hand on my lower back and a feathery touch just below my right shoulder blade. She was indicating the larger mole on my back. 'Come and palpitate it,' she ordered him, and I felt the heavier touch of the young man stretching and prodding around my shoulder-blade. He was much more confident handling me now he was safely away from my groin and he spent some time investigating my upper back. I could feel my erection ebbing away and I began to hope that I wouldn't have to worry about it when the time came to stand up at the end of the examination.

'Well, what is it?' she repeated.

He went quiet for a moment and then said. 'I'm not sure. I've gone blank.' At that point I realised that the whole experience must have been just as hard for him as it was turning out to be for me. I had arrived in the office wearing the full dress uniform of a respectable academic and been greeted with the titles Professor and Doctor. I was obviously socially quite comfortable with Dr Mercedes and spoke to her with the ease of a university colleague. He must have noticed me beaming charm towards her. The student could not know what type of Professor I was but the poor soul had been expecting simply to look at a fully healed scar on my left arm. Instead my naked body was suddenly and unexpectedly transformed into a teaching aid for the diagnosis of skin conditions in intimate regions. No wonder he was struggling to maintain a professional demeanour whilst trying to identity conditions he was not expecting to be tested on whilst wondering whose body he was fiddling with. But Dr Mercedes hadn't finished with him, or me, yet.

She stood by my left side and used my naked back with its various little imperfections to show her student examples of different types of basal cell papillomas. Towards the end of her lesson she stood by my right hip and rested a hand lightly on the base of my spine. The causal draping of her hand on the lower part of my back felt physically arousing. As far as I was concerned there was no particular loss of dignity in having my flaccid sexual organs inspected by an attractive mature women and her pretty female assistant in the presence of another male, but I would not have been comfortable if the young man had seen me develop an erection. Dr Mercedes had carefully shielded me from this potentially embarrassing situation without any fuss.

From the viewpoint of the student and the nurse she was simply using her hand to screen the top of my exposed buttocks from their view but the reassuring little squeezes she gave my lower back every now then, as she described the different sort of moles scattered over my back, felt very comforting, she was reassuring me that there was nothing to worry about in my large selection of blemishes.

When she had finished she turned round to block the view of the others and patted me on the bottom.

'Thank you.' she said. She stood between me and student as I rolled over to sit on the couch. I decided against adjusting my underwear, as to do so might easily have freed my erection to betray me. Dr Mercedes smiled a warm smile that began in her eyes and spread down her face as she said.

'You've nothing to worry about. All the lesions you showed me are benign. And I'm pleased with the way your arm has healed so I'm going to discharge you.'

Then she flashed a mischievous look at my bulge, which she was still shielding from the others' view. 'You're quite sure there's nothing else you'd like me to look at?' she said.

'I think I've shown you everything I ought to.' I smiled ruefully at her, red-faced but grateful that she was standing between me and the student.

'Thank you doctor,' I said. I didn't attempt to pull my underpants up. What would have been the point. It would just have drawn attention to my condition.

'Is there anything else you want to ask me about?' Dr Mercedes said.

'No,' I replied, 'You've dealt with everything that concerned me. Thank you again for everything.'

'You can sit there.' she said. I was grateful for that because it meant I could hide the evidence of my condition as the others left me to dress.

She walked out through the connecting door followed by her student and the nurse. When they had gone I jumped up and reached for my shirt but before I could grab it I heard someone come back into the room.

I hadn't pulled up my pants and my erection had not subsided. It was covered with fabric, but still obvious. The nurse stood there holding out my tweed jacket and the ipad which I had left in Dr Mercedes's office.

'Thank you,' I said, smiling at her. She didn't make eye contact but kept her gaze directed down, below my waist level. As I took my jacket she realised that I had registered that she was staring at the bulge in my underpants.

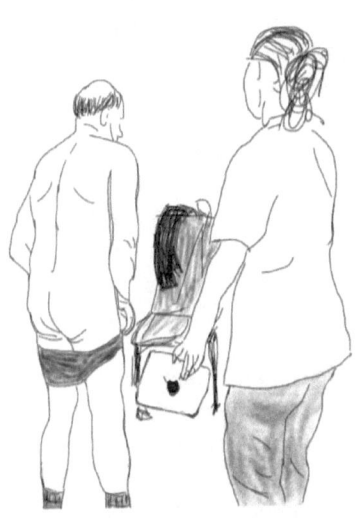

This was a chance to see if embarrassment could be averted by the exposed individual acting normally. I pretended to be unaware I was displaying signs of arousal. I tried charm to see if it could work for an semi-naked man with a not quite hidden erection.

'I see Dr Mecedes didn't hide my ipad while I was undressed,' I said and smiled again. This time she smiled back but didn't hold my gaze.

I had reminded her as she passed me the jacket that I was really a respectable academic, even if this was not reflected in my present inadvertently indecent demeanour.

Had we been on the street she would have run away from me to call the police, but in the context of the hospital my exposure was legal and acceptable, even if highly intimate. Had I been wearing trousers my embarrassing erection would not have been visible but wearing only briefs there was no hiding it. I turned around, leaned over to hang my jacket over the chair. She could see my bare bottom and from the corner of my eye I see she simply stood staring at me. She seemed to want to say something. As I straightened up and faced her I pulled up my briefs, pretending I had just noticed they were still pushed down so far and then reached for my ipad.

'Excuse me,' I apologised. It was a test of her ability to disregard. She passed it.

'When you're dressed,' she said, 'you can leave through this door. The doctor doesn't need to see you again.' I thanked her. This time she made eye-contact without glancing down. She went back into Dr Mercedes's office and closed the door.

I dressed and left, without seeing her, or Dr Mercedes, again.

Luckily I didn't find the experiment too embarrassing to handle and Dr Mercedes was charming and professional. But I had not foreseen that I might become aroused.

I would have been far more embarrassed if the young male student had seen my erection but I was less uncomfortable about Dr Mercedes seeing me in a state of arousal. She had clearly been amused. But she didn't embarrass me in front of the young man and she took the trouble to reassure me when dealing with my real fears about skin cancer. She checked all the blemishes before she used me as a teaching aid and I am quite sure that had any proved dangerous she would not have turned me into a visual aid for her student.

I had not foreseen that she would take advantage of the opportunity to use my body to teach her student how to recognise common benign skin lesions. But she also showed great consideration and treated me as a real person during that impromptu lesson. She kept touching me and making eye contact to reassure me that there was nothing serious to worry about. And she shielded my involuntary arousal from the view of the student.

I was surprised that I became aroused during the examination as I thought I was good at controlling myself. I hadn't expected Dr Mercedes to palpitate my pubic area and I never foresaw that she would keep her hand resting on my lower back, to reassure me as she used me as a teaching aid.

I found the experience of the examination exhilarating and scary. Totally unexpected things had happened. But I left the hospital on a mental high. I had been reassured about my health and had been able to observe the medical process of professional disregard at first hand. This experiment had thrown up a lot of unexpected information about the nature of myself, the way my body reacts to other people and the different ways people react to me when I am clothed and when I am naked.

I now understood what a tremendous transfer of power took place once I was undressed while she retained the uniform of a doctor. If I had been dressed I could have easily concealed any evidence of arousal. But whilst I was naked she could see exactly what was happening to me. My potential humiliation in front of the medical student was entirely in her gift, she could have stood aside and let the student see I was hard. I had taken a risk to gain knowledge and I had been lucky to escape being publicly embarrassed. With a less considerate doctor it could have been a far less enjoyable experience and could have easily resulted in humiliation, rather than exaltation.

A quick scan of the Internet on the subject of erections during medical examination yielded statistics from other lady dermatologists which claimed about 5% of men, i.e. about 1 in 20, get an erection during a naked skin check. As about half the patients will be women that means about 1 in every 40 patients gets hard for the doctor. It must be common enough to been seen regularly yet rare enough to be of note. I wondered if I been the subject of ribald comment between the nurse and Dr Mercedes about how easy I was to arouse? The nurse's use of 'the indiscreet glance' suggested that Dr Mercedes might have sent her back quickly to see me in order to add to the amusement value of an otherwise heavy day.

When took advantage of this opportunity to experience nudity in a medical situation I thought that the context would not be in any way erotic and would have no sexual overtones. I deliberately set out to test how the feelings and behaviour of that thing I call 'me' was affected by the suspension of the normal rules of modesty, embarrassment and clothing. I had two main objectives of study during the examination.

The first was to test the hypothesis that the etiquette of disregard would act to protect me from feeling shame and embarrassment when I was the only person in the room without clothing and the other was to test how powerful a tool a uniform is for interacting with other people.

What I hadn't bargained for was the presence of a young male, in the form of a medical student and there had been another surprise in store for me when I became involuntarily aroused during the procedure.

I thought that an extra observer wouldn't make any difference to my feelings and responses, but I was wrong. Having an additional younger male looking at my naked body did effect the dynamic of my feelings but not in a way I was expecting. I had reasoned that once all the observers had seen me naked then it wouldn't be a big deal for another male to take part in the examination. But I hadn't considered that there are more sensitive levels of exposure when standing naked before a member of same sex than there are with a member of the opposite sex. And as things developed I did become concerned about just what degree of nakedness the male observer might see. Again this came down to the fact that before the examination I was totally confident that I would be able to stay in control of my body and mind, without needing the emotional support of a uniform. But when it came to the crunch I realised that there are degrees of exposure which I find acceptable in front of a woman that are definitely embarrassing in front of a man. Without doubt, developing an erection is in that category. It's a natural thing to happen in front of a woman but not something I was comfortable revealing to a man.

When I was involuntarily aroused and couldn't stop it I felt vulnerable. To expose my erect member before a man would offer me up for humiliation. This is why I, along with most males, much prefer females to perform intimate procedures on me. I have an excuse for bodily responses in that case which is not available when being examined by a male.

Before this experiment I never doubted that I could control the physical responses of my body language so that it would send only the messages I intended it to. I thought of my body as a machine I could control by the actions of my conscious mind. To me it was like sailing a radio controlled power boat. My mind moved the control levers of the radio transmitter and the motors and servos of my muscles and sinews moved it exactly as I directed them. If I wished to undress then my limbs would carry out the necessary motions to remove as many clothes as I choose. If I wished to lie still and passive while Dr Mercedes examined me that is exactly what

I expected to happen. I am well practised in the use of body language and rhetoric to control students. But without the protection of clothing my conscious control mechanisms did not work as I expected. It was not like controlling a model power boat, the control process had changed to something that was much more like piloting a model yacht in a gusty and unpredictable wind. My mind could still move the levers to set the rudder and the sails but the movement of the vessel was also affected by changes in the wind. In those conditions the yacht can move in unexpected ways. The force of the wind is more powerful than the control mechanisms my transmitter can influence, so the boat makes movements beyond my control.

So it was with my body. My mind had intentions, and I knew how to use posture and position to convey messages but without the cover of clothing I was subject to other forces. These were not the psychogenic forces of mind and imagination I was familiar with as mechanisms of sexual arousal, but were reflexogenic and quite beyond my control. I had not realized how strongly involuntary arousal can become manifest during the conjunction of the formal uniform of the medical staff and the intimate nudity of the patient. How male models avoid accidental arousal when posing for female artists is something I had not considered before, after all Winston had told me that being naked for Deborah was an incentive for him to model and he never became erect.

Before this experiment I had not thought about involuntary erections. To me an erection was something that happened when I showed sincere interest in an attractive woman. I inclined to the view expressed by Alain de Botton who said.

'The stiffness of a penis is emotionally so satisfying and so erotic, because it signals a kind of approval that lies utterly beyond rational manipulation. Erections simply cannot be effected by willpower and are therefore particularly true and honest indices of interest. In a world in which fake enthusiasms are rife, in which it is often hard to tell whether people really like us or whether they are being kind to us merely out of a sense of duty, the stiff penis functions as a unambiguous agent of sincerity.'

As I had been expecting to go into a non-erotic situation with two professional women. I did not consider I might become aroused. But in addition to a voluntary intended erection there is another type that can arise from the chaotic chemical process known as my endocrine system.

As well as the familiar psychogenic erection caused by my brain voluntarily processing sensory, visual, auditory stimuli or fantasies to encourage my cortical centres to signal the sacral erection centres to release chemical messengers into my blood stream there is also the subversive reflexogenic erection. A reflexogenic erection is quite independent of what my mind is thinking. I later found that it is such a powerful instinct that this erection response can remain intact even after in men suffering cervical or thoracic spinal cord injuries. It is triggered by manual stimulation of nerve endings on various part of the body. The preganglionic neurons that signal my penile blood vessels are part of my spinal cord. The location of the parasympathetic erection centre is high up on my spine and I can influence it with my thoughts. The sympathetic erection centre is situated towards the base of my spine and is beyond the control of my mind. Starting from either of these locations in my spinal cord, voluntary or involuntary erectile triggers pass through the inferior hypogastric plexus via the cavernous nerves to the erectile tissue. But my mind can only block one of these mechanisms, the other is like the gusty wind blowing my model yacht where it will.

What I did not expect, before embarking on this little test, was that tactile stimulation of certain parts of my autonomic nervous system would cause me to have an erection whether I choose to have one or not. All my past experience of tactile stimulation and erections have been where have been an active participant in the process and have wanted to become hard. As I had never tried to stop this process I had not realized that it was not possible. What I learned from this experiment is there are circumstances when I am voluntarily naked and there is nothing I can do to stop my penis swelling and rising to the occasion.

Clothes perform a practical function as well as an emotional one. No matter how flimsy, they reduce the feeling of vulnerability. I now knew this feeling of helplessness was much stronger when I was naked. Clothes make the nerves in the surface of the skin less susceptible to triggering the release of nitric oxide, a key factor in increasing the blood flow to the penis. They also mask partial tumescence. Without clothing the skin is far more sensitive to the light touch of the doctor's fingers on it, and even slight arousal is clearly signalled by the change in angle of the penis. Any increase in girth, length and retraction of the foreskin only confirms the reaction. Once I was erect I was far more naked than when I was flaccid.

Author Phillip Carr-Gomm writes, 'The genitals have always represented the final frontier of nakedness You are only fully naked when your genitals are exposed. But for the male, the most significant boundary of that frontier is if he is seen erect.'

I agree with that. I was not uncomfortable exposing my genitals but I did not want the student to see me erect. That would have made me far too naked.

A week or so later I found I would soon be forced to test the validity of Carr-Gomm's statement. Dr Mercedes sent me go back to my GP to have the skin tag by my testicles removed. The GP made me an appointment with the practice nurse for the minor operation which would be done with a local anaesthetic and he called the nurse 'she'.

This time I was nervous at the prospect. My reaction to being touched by Dr Mercedes had shown me I might not be able to avoid physical arousal.

To have an erection in front of a nurse will be embarrassing so I have every incentive to prevent it. If a reaction still happens it can only be because my brain, is unable to control a reflexogenic arousal.

I arrived in good time to find the doctor's surgery empty apart from the receptionist. I signed into the arrival computer at 1:25 and sat down to wait. I was wearing smart academic summer clothes, a white sports jacket, gray trousers, short sleeved sports shirt and white suede shoes. The appointed time of 1:30 arrived and nothing happened. I waited and worried about what was going to happen.

Another five minutes passed. I was pretending to read a magazine to pass the time and all the while I was rehearsing in my mind what was about to happen. I had not yet seen the nurse but within a few minutes I was going to remove all clothing from the waist down and stand in front of her. It was now five minutes after the consultation should have started and I was still waiting to meet her. I could feel butterflies fluttering in my stomach again, as I wondered what she would be like and how I was going to feel during the test. I had sat there for another ten minutes before a slim lady of about fifty-something years of age, wearing severe glasses, a nurse's tunic and short pixie-cut hair appeared in the door way.

'Maurice Cowley?' she asked.

'Yes,' I said stepping forward.

'I'm Nurse Testarossa, Come this way,' she said, leading me along a corridor to a room marked Minor Surgery. She moved the sign on the door from Vacant to In Use.

Inside the room there was a couch, covered with a paper sheet, and table with some medical paraphernalia and a chair. She closed the door. She stood facing me. I smiled at her. She didn't smile back.

'You've come to have a skin tag removed?' she said.

'Yes, ' I said.

'Has the doctor explained the procedure to you?' she asked.

'Yes,' I said, 'I've had other tags removed from my arm and chest in the past. It's just that this one is in a more delicate area.'

She looked at me with a professional stare.

'It's here,' I said pointing to my groin. Her expression didn't change as she looked where I was pointing.

'Shall I undress and let you see it?' I asked.

'I'll get you a towel to cover yourself,' she said.

''There's no need to bother, really,' I said. 'you're a nurse and you need to have access to the area to remove the tag.'

'All right,' she said, 'if you're comfortable.'

Once I had agreed to undress for her she did not

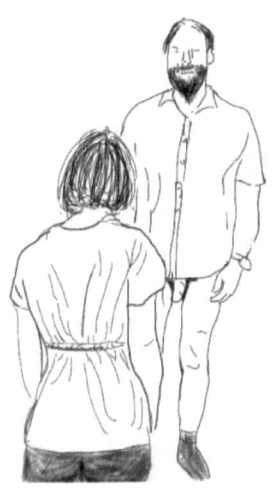

move me in a separate room as Dr Mercedes had done, but stood watching me as I removed my jacket and hung it over the back of the chair. I removed my trousers and folded them neatly also over the back of the chair. I did not feel uncomfortable about undressing in front of her and I did not feel any sense of eroticism as she watched me.

'The tag is inside the leg of my underpants and it catches and pulls sometimes,' I said, as I removed them, folded them carefully and placed them on my trousers.

I stood before her wearing just my socks and a short sleeved shirt which was too short to cover my genitals. All the protection of my clothing had gone. She could see my naked legs and pubic area but her expression had not changed. It was exactly the same expression she had shown when I was fully dressed. My penis was not showing any sign of arousal, in fact as I glanced down I thought it looked a little shriveled.

'Here it is,' I said and lifted my shirt, and held my testicles to one side to show her where the tag was. She learned forward and looked at me before straightening up and pulling on a pair of rubber gloves.

'Would you like to lie over here,' she said, indicating the couch with a rubber coated index finger.

I moved over to the couch, conscious that I was showing my naked buttocks to the nurse.

I lay down on my back and spread my legs exposing my groin area. The nurse stood next to me and looked at the skin tag.

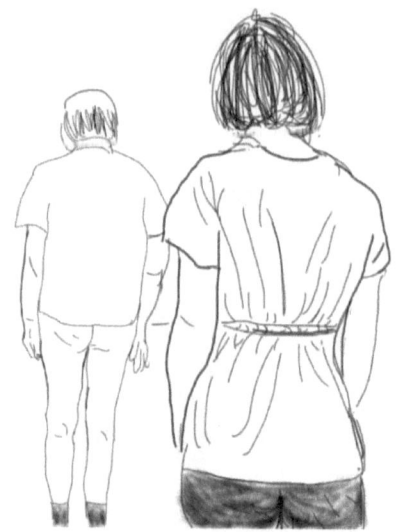

'I'm going to give you an injection,' she said, 'but first I'll just make you more comfortable.' She went to the table and ripped a small strip of paper off the roll used for covering the couch and laid it over my left leg and genitals. It was a small gesture towards modesty which didn't hide anything from her view. I could still see my genitals and so could she. However, it would have preserved my modesty if anyone else had entered the room, so it was a thoughtful gesture.

I felt a gentle touch on my right testicle as she held it to one side.

'You'll feel a little scratch,' she said as she inserted a needle into my inner thigh.

'I'll just think beautiful thoughts,' I said. She took out the needle and straightened up. As she did the paper modesty shield slid off. She didn't bother replacing it and I didn't ask her to.

'Which doctor are you with?' she asked, and smiled at me for the first time.

'Dr Jensen,' I replied.

'Have you had this tag for long?' she said.

'About six months.' I said. 'I'd hoped it would drop off by itself but it didn't.'

'I don't think it's anything to worry about.' she said. 'The local anesthetic won't take long.'

She went over to the table and picked up another instrument. I glanced down, my now exposed penis was looking a little plump. It was lying just a little proud of my belly, but I didn't feel, stimulated.

I hadn't felt any sense of arousal when the nurse had handled my testicles, there had been none of the sensual thrill I felt when Dr Mercedes's bare hands had rested on my lower back, but I could see I was slightly larger than I had been when I first dropped my underpants. The plumper appearance of my penis suggested that the nurse's touch on my testicles had triggered a release of nitric oxide into my blood stream, enough to increase the blood flow to my penis but not enough to make me erect.

The nurse returned with the cauterizer in her hand. She reached down towards my thigh.

'Can you feel anything?' she asked.

'No,' I replied. Then I felt her fingers brush my scrotum gently aside and grip my testicles for a moment. 'I can feel that.' I said.

I can feel you holding my balls I thought, worried that the anesthetic hadn't yet taken effect. But I didn't say anything and whilst I was worrying I felt a slight prickling on my thigh and smelt a whiff of burnt flesh. I winced slightly and felt my penis quiver as the muscles of my groin contracted.

'There,' the nurse said, 'it's all done.' She looked down. 'It isn't even bleeding.'

'That was quick,' I said, sitting up, opening my legs wide and holding my scrotum to one side to get a clear view of the wound.

'I don't think it needs a dressing,' she said looking more closely at the site. 'You'll just have a little scab which will fall off in a few days.'

'If you think it doesn't need a plaster then I'm ok about it,' I said as we both studied my naked groin. I felt confident that I'd managed to control myself.

'How big was the tag?' I asked.

'No bigger than this,' she said, as she reached over and showed me the tag, now sitting in a little specimen jar.

'It felt much bigger when it was part of me.' I said.

'I'll send it off for testing,' she said, 'but I think it's quite harmless. You can get dressed now.' And she looked down and smiled a knowing little smile at me. I followed her gaze and on the paper cover just beneath my penis I could see a slight damp patch. I hadn't got an erection when she touched my testicles but I had been affected enough to ooze Cowper's fluid and the evidence for this was obvious from the sheen on the tip of my penis. I stood up quickly and moved over to the chair where my clothes were. The nurse followed me. She stood faced me and chatting about skin tags as I began to dress.

'That was really quick and easy,' I said while I unfolded my underpants and held them open ready to step into. 'I was a little nervous about letting someone with a knife loose between my legs.' I put my right leg into my underpants, looked up at her and smiled. 'But you were really very gentle.'

'That's alright', she said. She smiled back and was quite obviously watching me dress.

I lifted my left leg into my underpants and pulled them up.

'Thank you,' I said as I adjusted my pants comfortably around my crotch.

'It's quite an easy procedure and doesn't hurt.' she continued 'You might get some discomfort when the local wears off, but if you do just take a paracetamol.'

I stepped into my trousers, pulled them up, fastened my belt and zipped my fly shut. She was still watching me as I pulled on my jacket, put on my shoes and completed my metamorphosis back into a respectable academic.

'Thank you nurse,' I said as I shook her still gloved hand.

This encounter revealed some surprising and unexpected insights. The nurse had shown perfect control of the etiquette of disregard whilst I was undressed and had not commented in any way at the dripping evidence of autonomous reflexive arousal which her handling of my testicles had evoked. She had carried on a normal conversation with me while I clambered into my underpants but she had not hidden her natural curiosity about how I dressed my naked body. She had only relaxed enough to smile at me once I demonstrated I was not embarrassed to reveal my private parts to her.

I did not get an erection, because the tactile stimulation was so fleeting, but I was not able to prevent seepage of Cowper's fluid from my penis. The nurse had not said anything but she had noticed what was happening. This was a perfect example of professional etiquette of disregard in operation. It does, however, confirm my suspicion that there are a lot of bodily functions that I cannot control, no matter how hard I try. Clothing would have disguised the give-away sign of arousal which the seepage of pre-seminal fluid betrayed to the nurse.

I have to conclude that Phillip Carr-Gomm hasn't told the whole story about the frontier of nakedness. Revealing my genitals whilst retaining some clothing did not make me feel naked. I didn't feel too vulnerable while I still had a shirt on. I think I needed the token cover of the paper towel, which for all practical purposes only concealed my genitals from any intruder but left them visible to the nurse. What I wasn't aware of at the time was that when she had swabbed around my perineum and held my scrotum, to keep my testicles out of the way, she had activated my subversive reflexogenic arousal system. She had unintentionally stimulated my Cowper's gland which responded by releasing viscous fluid from my urethra. I believed I had controlled myself and was not aware of the revealing drips until the nurse draw my attention to them whilst carefully not mentioning the matter. However, her body language clearly showed that she was aware and possibly amused.

Phillip Carr-Gomm is correct when he says that that you cannot hide your responses while your genitals are exposed.

These experiences with the medical profession had convinced me that there is a considerable imbalance of power between a dressed person and an undressed one which has to be handled with great care. Clothing does hide many inadvertent bodily signals and removing our clothes makes it impossible to keep even subtle reactions private.

I had taken every mental precaution to avoid the embarrassment of an involuntary erection and thought I had succeeded, only to discover that tactile stimulation of the nerves in my groin and perineum area had stimulated my Cowper's gland to cause my apparatus to begin its cycle of preparation for sex. I was able to hold off having an erection because the stimulation was fleeting, so the time delay for the build-up of nitric oxide in my bloodstream had not reached the tipping point, before the stimulation ceased. Had it gone on longer then I might have become erect and once again been forced across that final frontier of naked exposure.

Chapter 10: A Secret Social Theatre

Life-drawing is distinct from other practices of bodily display or performance (such as sex-entertainment), and is probably better understood as a type of collaborative performance of a collection of actants, rather than the performer/audience model. It is popular as a social theatre in which exhibitionism and voyeurism can be explored in a number of settings that are controlled and relatively safe for all participants. - Margaret Mayhew

After my unnerving experiences whilst exploring the medical etiquette of the disregard of nakedness I had a far better insight into the issues faced by the models in life drawing classes. I had been suspicious about the balance of power between the clothed artists and the nude models ever since I had been encouraged to take up life drawing. Now I knew from practical experience just how vulnerable it feels to be naked in the company of clothed people, even if they are trained medical professionals.

The rituals of the life drawing studio are there to reduce the models' sense of jeopardy and encourage them to undertake the somewhat cold and uncomfortable work. By becoming naked they deliberately place themselves in a position that would normally be interpreted as sexual availability. But letting someone see you naked is not the same as having sex with them, and is not an offer to engage in sexual intercourse.

I wondered why some people, such as Eileen, seemed to enjoy being models, whilst others such as Pauline, modelled only as a favour, or in the case of Deborah, as a duty, on condition they remained dressed.

On at least three occasions during the teaching schedule Deborah had been let down by models and been forced to find substitutes, first Pauline in a bathing suit, then June in an exhibitionist flurry and later herself fully clothed. The motivation of models was not as simple as it had seemed at first. Certainly they were paid, but not much. I was becoming curious about what motivated individuals to model. Then, suddenly, it looked as though I might never find out.

The course Deborah had been teaching was finishing, the local evening centre where it was held was to be closed and the building sold for conversion into flats. If I wanted to keep drawing I needed to find another course, or a new source of models.

I asked Deborah if she knew of any other classes where I could go to continue practising drawing.

'I run a life drawing group at my own studio,' she said. 'I don't teach them. We just share the cost of a model and I provide the studio space. You're welcome if you'd like to come along. We meet on Wednesday evenings.'

'That sounds ideal,' I said, and that is how I joined Deborah's life drawing group.

I arrived in good time at the venue, and recognised the deconsecrated ex-Chapel. I had thought the address sounded familiar and that was because the address was that of the Methodist Sunday School I had attended as a child. Now it had been converted into a house and studio. As I stood outside I had a flashback to attending every Sunday afternoon, and being told to keep myself pure in thought and mind.

I went through the familiar Gothic front door into what had been the main hall, and saw it was now partitioned into a much smaller studio and living space. There were three men and Deborah inside. Deborah greeted me and told me how things were organised, where the brewing facilities were and how to find the loo. She introduced one of the men as her husband, Jack and told me he was also an artist and a regular patron of the life-drawing group.

As I sorted out my drawing pads and pencils a young woman came in and said 'Hello'.

She was wearing denim jeans and a denim jacket over a sweater. She had long brown hair which was drawn back into a tight bun on the back of her head. The studio was warm and comfortable. It was well lit and had plenty of easels, chairs and drawing boards. There were two rooms off the studio, one contained the tea brewing equipment and the loo, and had a closed communication door to the living quarters. The other had a set of sliding doors which were open. The woman went through to the side room, leaving the doors open, and undressed. She made no attempt to keep out of sight and stood naked with her back to the main room as she folded her clothes I caught a glimpse of her bare bottom through the door and even though she would soon to stand voluntarily naked before me I felt a guilty thrill of forbidden voyeurism at seeing her statuesque backside with its fleshy buttocks.

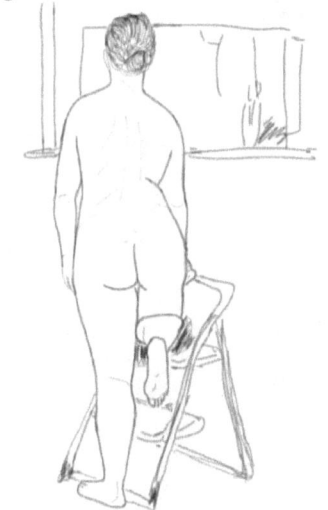

She finished folding her clothes and put on a knee length robe and a pair of slippers. She walked across the studio and into the utility room to come out clutching a mug of tea, a few minutes later.

Deborah suggested that Maureen, which was the name of the model. did a series of quick poses to help us get our eye in.

Maureen removed her robe without hesitation. She took up the first pose which was a standing one, with one leg raised onto the chair. I quickly sketched the line of her back, buttocks and legs. I had no sense of voyeurism as I drew her now. I had felt guilty when I had stolen that glimpse of a private region of her body when she had not been aware I was looking. Now she was willingly displaying the same area for me to draw that sense of guilt evaporated.

After ten minutes Deborah told Maureen to rest. She remained naked while she stretched and eased her muscles. She undid the bun from her hair and shook it out making no attempt to conceal her genitalia or her neatly trimmed pubic hair.

Deborah next placed her on a low stool in a sitting pose with her back towards me. After five minutes, when Deborah called for a change of pose, Maureen stood up, stretched and then crouched down and bent over, letting her hair hang down. This

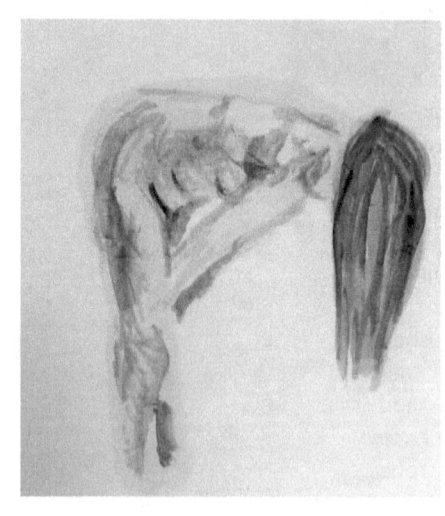

gave a nice line to her back and exposed the cleavage of her buttocks in an uninhibited way even though Jack, was drawing from directly behind her. I had a side view and her pose reminded me of the classic Egyptian drawings of the sky-goddess Nut.

When that short pose ended she stood up and put on her robe while Deborah discussed the next one, which was to be a longer standing pose. I was facing Maureen as she got into position and she made no attempt to hide her pubic region. She tried letting her arms hang down by her side but she must have felt exposed as she realised I would have been staring directly at her groin for the next twenty minutes. She lowered her arms across her belly so

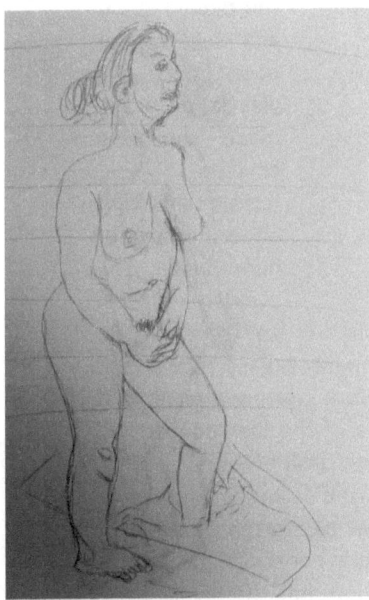

that her hands shielded her pubic region.

I spent a while looking at her, to work out the main proportions of the pose and she did not avoid my eye. Her body was perfectly still but her eyes were watching mine as though she was noting which part of her body I was looking at. When I looked back into her eyes she held my gaze without hesitation.

Halfway through the session we had a break and Maureen put her robe on, coiled her hair back into a tight roll, and wandered about, looking at the drawings and talking to the artists. Once she was wearing her robe she became a friendly art critic, and told me that she too was an artist, who also drew with the life group.

Deborah suggested to Maureen that the final pose should be a sitting one that would last for the final hour.

Once more Maureen put her arm across her belly

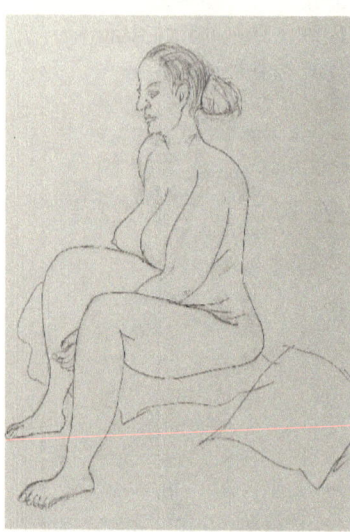

so that her arm shielded her genital slit. Although she did not bother to hide her labia as she moved about and set up her poses, once she was in pose she made sure she covered her female parts with either her arm or her hand. She avoided letting any of the male artists stare at her intimate organs while she modelled. She checked before starting a pose, well knowing that the etiquette of the life room would not allow her to adjust her position once in pose, not matter how uncomfortable she the artists to stare intently once she was comfortably settled. It was impossible for her to hide her sexual parts while she was moving into position, but she invoked the life room's etiquette of disregard during those revealing movements and we all pretended not to be looking. Once she stopped moving and froze into the still detachment of the pose we artists were not just allowed but encouraged to stare at what she showed us.

In three out of the five gesture poses she choose to display her backside. As Deborah only gave a broad indication of the quick poses she wanted, Maureen had the choice of facing towards or away from the artists.

She was far more coy about her genitals when in pose than June, the uninhibited artist/model I had

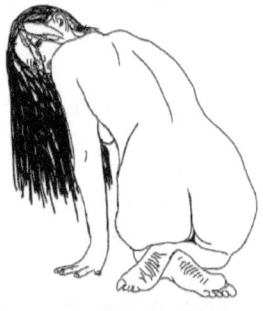

drawn at the night classes, but she was proud of her back view and whenever Deborah gave her freedom to choose she show-cased her rump freely.

She was happy to talk to the artists while she was wore her robe but would only speak to Deborah while nude. She made eye contact with the artists while she was in pose, but not while she was arranging her body to be viewed. Whilst naked and moving she kept her eyes down.

'Why do you life draw so regularly?' I asked Deborah at the end of the session.

'It helps me keep mentally fit,' she said. 'It exercises all the important creative aspects of my being and gives me the tools to explore other forms of drawing. I set up this group to force myself to draw at a fixed time and I book a model to make sure I take time to explore the figure. When I'm teaching a class I have to pay attention to the students. When I draw for myself I want total concentration. I go into a sort of self-generated altered state when I concentrate and then I feel the drawing flow. I can't get to this mental state if I'm disturbed by external events or student's issues. When I'm distracted I can't find the part of me that connects to what I'm seeing and how I feel about it. Even in this life group I have to keep a polite relationship with the other participants, and I struggle with this when I'm trying to move into my life drawing meditation mode. You might notice I don't communicate or pass opinions on your work as often I did when I was teaching you. You'll have to live with the fact that I'm into my own experience.'

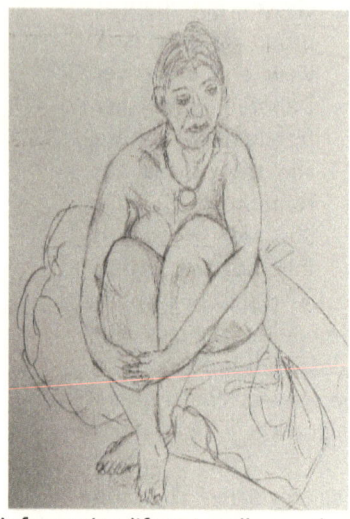

She smiled at me. 'Being an artist is a selfish solitary calling I'm afraid'

'What makes a good life drawing session for you?' I asked.

'It should be a sensory episode, with a sort of buzz in the air, I want to feel the veils of obscure and irrelevant information lift so I really see the model I'm drawing. It takes time and concentration to get to that point. I feel a sort of oneness between the marks I make, the model and myself. This focus keeps me fit and flexible. I force myself to work through the routines and discipline of practice and splice it with passion and interest. I have to enjoy the visual language of the materials I choose and understand the relative qualities of the surfaces I want to work with. I need the room to be right, with good space and not too crowded. I need to have good lighting qualities, I need to see the energy and character in the model.'

'Do you need to know the model well to be able to draw them as you want to?' I said. 'Is it easier to draw models who are friends or hired professionals?'

'I don't necessarily need to know the model but I know in the first few minutes when a model isn't right. A model I know well is rare and I'm not sure how to define that? How can you ever really know anyone? There has to be a professional distance. I'm friendly but I wouldn't class any of my models as friends although some I've worked with some for

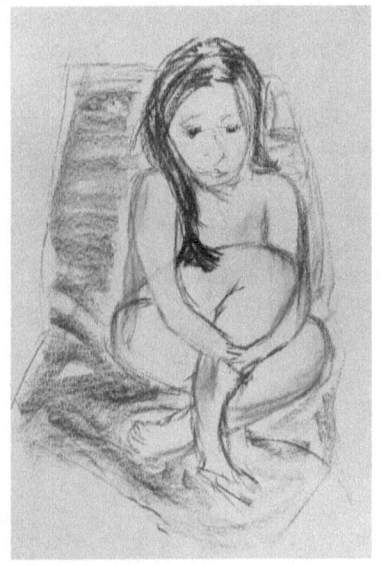

years and I love to draw them. The main thing for me is to trust that they will turn up on time and be interested in their role as model. Life drawing is a partnership between artist and model.'

'Do you prefer male or female subjects?' I said.

'I prefer to draw the female form,' she said. 'I often find the male figure uninspiring,'

She looked me up and down and grinned at me. 'Although my favourite model is a 75 year old retired hill famer on his 5th hip replacement. He's almost skeletal which makes him interesting to draw. There's a world of knowledge to be gleaned from a studio based relationship between artist and model.'

'Maurice,' she went on. 'Let me just advise you. I've noticed that you seem to be focus too much on your interior thoughts when you should to be reacting more freely to the model's exterior and dynamic. You need to develop your aesthetic sense and understanding of the human form. It's the key to the quality, viability and variability in your drawing. You need to empathise more with the model'.

I'll keep working on it.' I said. 'See you next week.'

Over the next few weeks we had other models, who Deborah used regularly and one was male.

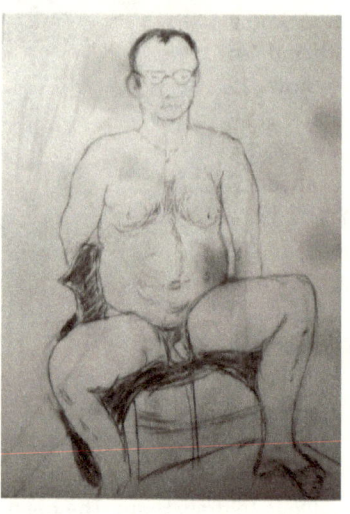

When Maureen wasn't modelling she came along as an artist to draw. Her drawings were lively and interesting and she had a natural empathy with the other models.

I soon noticed how different each model was in the way they approached their role.

One model, whom I will call Joan, was an articulate lady of about forty who was quick to commit to open revealing poses, unlike Maureen. She was not bothered about the difference between being in pose and being naked.

The first time she sat for the group, she was already in her robe when I arrived. At seven o'clock prompt, she took off her robe and began to discuss what poses she should do with the whole group. She happily demonstrated possible positions of her body and asked for feedback on the postures she was trying before she committed to them. She was totally open about how difficult the pose might be to hold and how long she felt she would be able to keep still whilst in it.

When Deborah suggested that she try standing in front of a full length mirror, so that she showed an almost 360 degree image of herself she tried it at once. She was totally spontaneous with her body and wasn't bothered about talking to the artists while naked or moving about trying 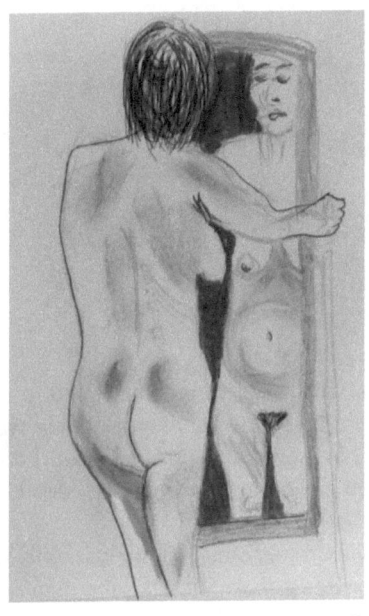 different positions. In fact she invited comments and suggestions to improve the pose.

When Joan was modelling the whole group was relaxed. She loved being naked so nobody felt uncomfortable about interacting with her to suggest poses which she could try out before she agreed to them. We artists could see exactly what the pose was going to look like and were able to suggest changes to make it more interesting while Joan was able to decide how difficult that body position would be to hold. She would say things like, 'I can keep this for 15 minutes, but not much longer,' before we started drawing. She was pretty good at estimating her endurance most of the time but there was one notable exception. She had a tendency to go to sleep in reclining poses.

If anyone at the university had suggested to me
before I retired, that I would enjoy spending

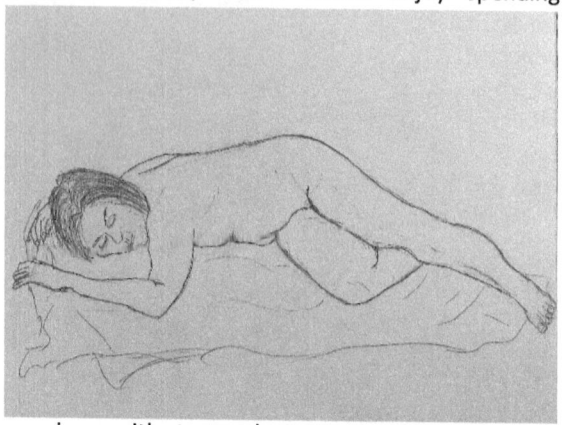

evenings with two other men and a couple of
women sitting round a naked sleeping woman and
drawing her body while she snoozed I would have
told them they were barmy. But here I was doing
just that and enjoying it.

What was remarkable about Joan was that if she
woke up after sleeping in pose she didn't move. The
only clue was that her eyes would open and her
breathing speed up.

'How do you manage to keep still when you wake
up?' I said.

'I know when I doze off I am in pose and so I tell
myself that when I wake up I must stay be in pose
and keep still,' she said.

I felt comfortable enough to ask her if she felt cold
while she was posing. She said that that when she
first removed her robe, the air felt cold on her skin
but her body adjusted to the air temperature during
the evening, but if the pose went on for a long time
then she started to feel colder, speculating this was
because her blood flow slowed if she wasn't moving.
But she couldn't have felt too cold because she
never bothered to put her robe back on at the end of

the sessions, she just walked out of the studio to the changing area still naked with her robe over her arm. She only used her robe to wait for the session to begin. Once it was off it never went back on. Joan enjoyed the nude role. When I asked her why she modelled she was quite open about it.

'When I'm naked I'm the centre of attention. I get to show my body to intelligent, fascinating people, who really appreciate the show I put on for them,' she said. 'And it gives me a chance to sit quietly and think, or to drift away into dreams, knowing that I am being totally honest about who I am. I literally have nothing to hide. I am the star of my own show.'

'Are you an artist too?' I said.

'Good heavens no.' she said, almost laughing at the suggestion. 'I'm not here to compete with people who can draw. I'm here to be drawn. I'm an object of art not a manufacturer of it.'

There was the difference between her and Maureen. Maureen was an artist who also modelled and she was totally conscious of the demands made on her. She controlled the views she displayed when she played the role of nude. Joan simply liked having her naked body admired and appreciated.

The boundary between the roles of artist and model in Deborah's life group were much less defined than they had been in her night school class. In class, the artists were amateur students and the models were professionals, paid to remove their clothes and keep still. Deborah was the teacher and fully in control. Here the group had a life of its own and many of its members moved between roles, as I found out one week.

I arrived at the chapel at quarter to seven and was first there. The other two regular male artists, arrived soon after me. Deborah came into the studio with the session programme mapped out until mid-

April. I checked out the room where the models changed. I now knew it was used as a spare bedroom with clear glass doors. It didn't afford the models much privacy to change which is how I had been able to snoop on Maureen undressing the first time I drew her. A trim young woman of about thirty-five came in. Deborah called her Jennie and seemed to know her well. As it was getting close to seven o'clock I wondered if she was to be our model but Deborah kept looking at her watch and watching the door.

'I've booked a male model.' She said, 'and he emailed to say he'd be coming but he's not turned up.'

At that moment Jack, Deborah's husband came in.

'The model's not turned up,' she said. 'Jack will you model?'

Jack looked at his watch. 'He's got three minutes yet.' He said. 'He might still turn up. I was hoping to do some drawing.' He sounded wistful and resigned. 'Can't you model?' he said to Deborah.

'Not tonight I need to do some studies of a male nude for a student project I have to teach. You'll have to do.' She said.

Jack is tall and thin, with spectacles and always wears a shirt and tie. He looks like a stereotype of an old fashioned geography teacher. All he needed to complete the image was a sports jacket with leather patches on the elbows.

'Go and get ready,' Deborah ordered, obviously worried that she had a group of artists assembled and no model for them to draw.

At this point a wild thought flitted through my mind. Should I should volunteer to stand in and model? I didn't need to strip, I could pose dressed, as Deborah had done. But I was the newcomer, so I kept quiet. Jack went into their living quarters and returned a couple of minutes later wearing a bathrobe and a pair of slippers.

'We'll do three short poses of about 20 minutes each and a longer pose to finish off.' Deborah said. 'We'll start with a sitting pose.'

Jack slipped off his gown, slippers and spectacles and stood waiting by the chair. He faced the artists naked and made no attempt to hide his sexual parts.

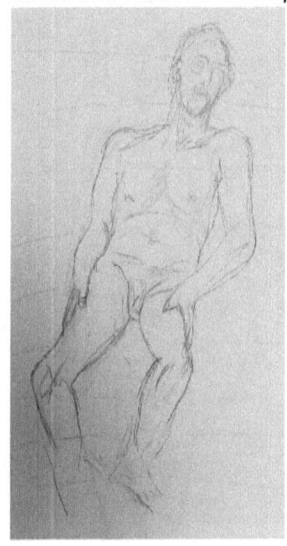

As Phillip Carr-Gomm said in his book, *A Brief History of Nakedness,* 'The genitals have always represented the final frontier of nakedness. You are only fully naked if your genitals are exposed.' Jack had crossed that frontier and been transformed from a figure of authority to a symbol of vulnerability in the shedding of a robe.

By removing his clothes Jack morphed from a scholarly, respectable unchallengeable authority figure into a simple, male animal.

He stepped forward, his penis swaying in sympathy with his body movements, and faced the group. When he spoke, he sounded friendly, assured and knowledgeable. He looked like any anonymous naked male but still sounded like a caring teacher. He asked if the group would like a simple pose or something foreshortened and complicated.

'Foreshortened please.' Deborah said. Jack pushed himself backwards into the models' chair with his knees apart, leaned slightly sidways and placed his hands alongside his thighs and his head on one side. He was lying back at an angle of about forty five degrees.

As I was sitting right in front of him his head looked out of proportion to his body and his torso was tremendously foreshortened.

We went through four poses that evening and for the final seated one he wore his glasses which made a strange juxta-position.

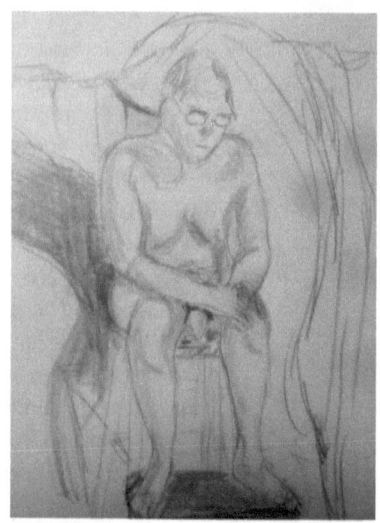

Jack chatted with the group as he got into pose. Once in pose he was still and quiet, but between poses he happily chatted away as he had done when he was dressed. He did, however, stay within the mod-elling area while he was naked. Only when we stopped for a tea break did he put on his robe and move about the room to look at the drawings.

At the end of the session I complimented him on how he managed to stay so still when in pose, and asked him how he managed it. He said that if he fidgeted then Deborah would get annoyed with him, so he kept quite motionless. He said it with a smile on his face.

I was finding the more I practiced the easier it was to draw and the more I liked what I drew. Deborah encouraged me to simplify my line and try to

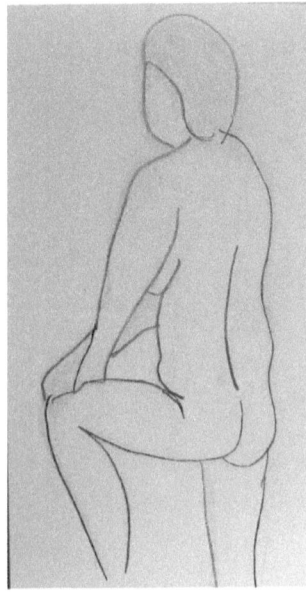

become more expressive with fewer, simpler lines.

'Drawing is a visual language,' she said. 'if you were learning Russian or Chinese or even hieroglyphics it would take time and practice with all the tools available to get to an good standard. Be kind to yourself, Maurice and enjoy the journey.' She winked at me. 'Experiment with revealing your soul.'

She suggested I should explore the pastel drawings of Odilon Redon's depicting Parsifal and think about the erotic tortured lines of an Egon Schiele figure drawing. She lent me books and I spent quite a few evenings studying how powerful simple lines could be.

What had most impressed me, since joining Deborah's life drawing group, was her continual message that drawing is about emotion, and the marks that artists make are a language to express feelings. I had also taken on board the idea that to improve my drawing I needed to take risks.

Deborah kept saying. 'An artist needs to put themselves in a place beyond their comfort zone, if they want to extend their experience and stretch their imagination'.

Both Maureen's and Jack's drawings had a sense of life and naturalness about them, which I could rarely see in my own drawings. I had come to the conclusion that they both knew more about the interaction between the artist and the model, than I did. There was something about this relationship that I did not understand and my drawings showed my lack of insight and sparkle.

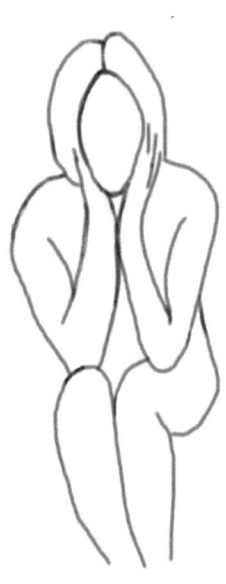

I was making maps of the topology of the model not interpreting the emotion or portraying the risks which the model took as part of their role.

I knew what a model looked like under the scrutiny an artist, but I didn't know how the model felt. This was something that Jack knew because he had shown that he was not only prepared to draw he would also pose. Winston had said that he liked to work on both sides of the easel, but preferred to model for female artists. I also noted that Deborah had not invited him to join her life drawing group. Perhaps he had let his exhibitionist tendency become just a little too obvious to be invited to join a private group which included Deborah's husband.

I was surprised to see that quite a few artists wanted to model in the nude as well as draw. Deborah had told me that Winston was modelling to help him improve his drawing skills. Was nude modelling the secret ingredient which added sparkle to an artist's work? Did a serious artist have to learn to stretch their comfort zone by modeling naked in order to draw well from life? But there was an exception to this rule I was hypothesizing. When Deborah had stood in for the missing model at the night class she had kept her clothes on, so perhaps it wasn't a general rule. Then something happened to change my mind.

A few weeks later when I arrived at Deborah's studio she was there with Jack and the two other guys who came regularly. She was looking at her iphone as I walked in.

'Maureen's just emailed to say she can't model tonight, she's been delayed at work.' She said.

'Does that mean we have to scrap this evening's group?' I said.

Deborah, looked at Jack. 'No', he said. 'I filled in last time a model let you down. It's your turn tonight.'

Deborah shrugged. 'OK,' she said. 'You lot set up while I go and change.' She was wearing a sloppy artist's smock over a pair of jeans.

She disappeared into their living quarters. I was expecting her to come back out wearing her night school teacher's uniform as she had done last time I had seen her take on the model's role, but she came back in a robe and slippers.

'What sort of pose do you fancy, Maurice?' she said. She must have put a bikini on, I thought, like Pauline had when she was roped in to pose.

'How about seated cross legged on the floor?' I said. 'And could you rest your chin on your right hand, like you did when I drew you when you stood in at night school.'

'Easy,' she said. 'Are the rest of you happy with that?' Jack and the other guys nodded. Deborah laid a padded exercise mat on the floor and spread a cover over it. She kicked off her slippers and shrugged out of her robe.

She hadn't been to put on a swim suit, she was naked. She squatted down, cross legged in a yogic lotus position with her left hand stretched out towards me turning her head to one side and supporting her chin with her right hand. She turned her eyes to look directly at me.

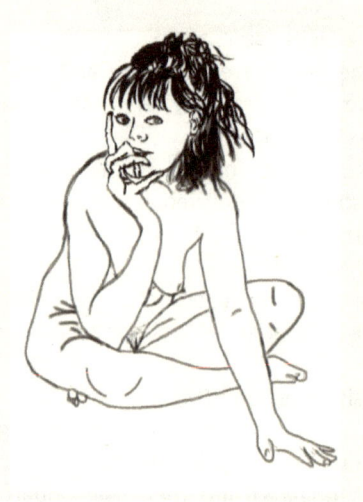

'How's that?' she said.

I gulped and nodded. For once I was lost for words.

'Look carefully, Maurice and draw everything you see,' she said in her primmest school teacher's voice. 'I don't want to see any false modesty in your drawing'.

I did draw exactly what I saw, right down to the detail of her shaved lower belly. Deborah had none of Maureen's coyness in pose now she was the model.

'I can hold this for about 30 minutes,' she said. 'Will someone time it please?'

'I will.' Jack said. 'Time starts now.'

178

Deborah sat perfectly still and composed, and watched me draw. I knew full well that she expected me to pay full attention to all each and every part of her body, including her reproductive regions, which she was not hiding. She followed that pose with a half hour standing one with her arms folded above

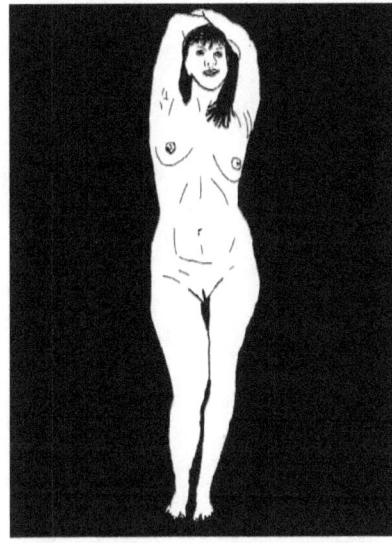 her head. She stood against a black back drop to create a really vivid image.

When we stopped for a break she put on her robe, and Jack made her a cup of tea.

She stood beside me, sipping her

tea and looked at my two drawings.

'You made a better likeness of my face in the seated pose but I like the drama of your second drawing.' she said. 'It has a nice line to it and using the black ground to make the silhouette of my body stand out works well.' She grinned at me. 'But you haven't concentrated on my facial features as well as you did in the seated pose. I can see myself in that sitting portrait whilst in the standing pose you've turned me into any anonymous female.'

'It's odd really,' I said. 'While nakedness reveals everything about your body it also makes you anonymous. Once undressed you look like every other naked woman unless you interact with me. You weren't looking directly at me in the standing pose, but you were in the seated one. That's why in the seated pose I responded to Deborah, not just a nude model.'

She giggled. 'Yes I was deliberately staring at you during the first pose, I was watching your face. It was a wonderful mixture of curiosity and guilt.'

'You surprised me', I said. 'I expected you to stay dressed, like you did for the night class.'

'Surprised you or shocked you?' she said.

'I just wasn't expecting you to pose nude for me.' I said.

'Why wouldn't I be prepared to do exactly what I ask any model to do for me?' she said. 'We're all artists learning together here. Not a teacher and her students. In this group I don't need to keep a professional distance for the sake of the local authority's good name. Here I can be completely myself.'

'What do you have planned for your final long pose,' I said.

'I'll do a really anonymous back view for you for in the long pose,' she said. 'Provided you won't be shocked.'

'I promise to enjoy drawing your bum,' I said, smiling broadly. 'And I won't be shocked.'

'You may as well admit that the main appeal of life drawing for you, and probably most male artists, is a sublimated and tightly controlled sexual tension that you experience when you draw a naked model,' Deborah said. 'Particularly a woman you never expected to see without clothes.'

'I haven't really analyzed drawing as a form of spectatorship.' I said.

'Well that's what it is.' Deborah said. 'I've always believed that complete nudity in front of my fellow artists brings us closer together. You now know a lot more about me than you did before I stood naked before you. But nudity can disrupt and confuse the boundary between students and teaching staff. It's important when teaching a night school class to maintain appropriate relationships with students for ethical reasons.'

'I suppose you're really talking about the boundaries between your public and private persona,' I said. 'When you're employed as a teacher you must maintain a certain distance to be respected. Appearing naked in front of your students would make you vulnerable and unable to maintain authority and discipline in class. But here you are just one artist among kindred spirits.'

'You're beginning to understand.' She said, 'modelling and drawing are two sides of the same coin. To be a complete artist you must know and understand both sides of the creative relationship. You've got to be prepared to indulge in transgressive practices of acceptable naked display and permitted voyeurism.'

'I suppose we all have to negotiate our sexual, professional and creative boundaries.' I said.

'Yes,' Deborah said. 'I'm always conscious of the imbalance of power between the clothed artists and teacher, and the naked model.'

'I soon picked up on the etiquette of the life class and the need to respect the model's gift of posing for the sake of Art.' I said. 'It is a most peculiar privilege to be allowed to stare at the naked body of a stranger.'

'That protocol of the life room dates back to the Government Regulations of life modelling issued by Lord Chamberlin in 1851.' Deborah said.

'What did they say?' I said.

'That the room must be closed during the session, only artists could be allowed inside, the model had to remain completely still whilst disrobed. Students shouldn't talk to, or touch the model whilst in pose. Poses must be agreed with the model before they disrobe. When not posing the model must put on a robe.'

'Does that mean I shouldn't be talking to you while you are naked, except for your robe?' I said.

'There's nothing wrong with a polite chat with the model during a break, if she agrees to socialize, as I have. But the talk must be professional. You mustn't take advantage of a model's vulnerable state of dress to come on to her.' Deborah said. 'And you mustn't stare down inside her robe.'

'Sorry,' I said. 'I hadn't realized I was.'

'All men do it, even though you've just spent an hour looking at my naked body and in a minute or so you'll see it fully on show for an hour.' She said. 'The difference is that when I am in pose I have agreed to show you my body, but when I put on my robe I expect you to respect my modesty. There is a different between perving at my body without my consent and observing it to draw.'

'I think I get it.' I said. 'As a model you want to be looked at, but on your terms, not mine. Is that why you model?'

'I suppose at some level I do want to be looked at, but in a safe environment. Modelling is an empowering expression of sexuality. There are not many opportunities for naked display without the risk of physical or sexual contact. I can explore my inner sexual sensations without having to be responsible for the reactions of the observers.' Deborah said. 'If you model yourself, you soon learn how to behave properly with any models you employ as either an artist or a teacher, and what you can reasonably expect them to do in pose.'

'I suppose I'm taking part in a sort of social theatre,' I said. 'Where I can explore both exhibitionism and voyeurism in a setting that's controlled and safe for all the people who have consented to take part in it.' I said.

'Exactly,' Deborah said. 'But you've restricted yourself to voyeurism whilst I need to get back to practicing exhibitionism'.

With that she moved over to the modelling stand. Set up a pedestal, covered it with drapes, folded her robe, laid to one side and lay across the pedestal.

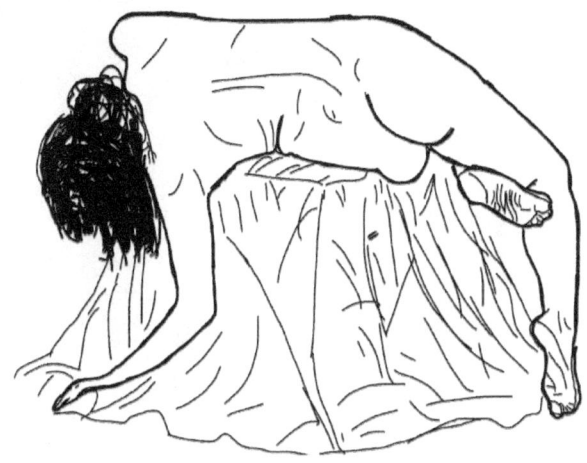

As I drew her back view I tried to convince myself that together Deborah and I were mutually engaged in creating Art.

She held the pose for almost an hour until Jack called time. Then she got up and stretched without putting on her robe.

'That was a difficult one,' she said, as she shrugged and shimmied the blood flow back into her limbs. Still naked, she stepped over and stood beside me, looking at my drawing for almost a minute.

I realized I was actually living out the fantasy I had imagined and rejected when Deborah had told her night school class she was going to stand in for the model who hadn't turned up. Deborah, my art teacher, was standing next to me, stark naked inspecting and commenting on my drawing.

'No bad, Maurice,' she said before strolling away to put on her robe. 'See you next week.'

Chapter 11: Tipping the Balance of Naked Power

The first thirty seconds of nudity are always the worse: sudden, shocking and unpredictable, jumping instead of tiptoeing into a cold sea. Human reactions can be unpredictable, and the artist can hurt you, make a face, a comment, a gesture that will come as a terrible shock to your system.
Kathleen Rooney-Model and Writer

There is one further step in understanding life drawing left for me to experience and that is to model. Can I do it?

The nude is the most complete visual symbol of a human being. There is no better illustration to accurately portray the human condition. Is that my fear? Am I too old? Unclothed before an artist I will have to confront my aging body.

To dare to model will put me in a revelatory situation. If I model for Deborah, who I know as teacher, mentor and model, will this intimate interaction give me a range of new insights?

The finished drawing will be permanent evidence of a shared experience of the exposure of my body. It will be an enduring record of the triangular relationship between artist, model and drawing medium, as we share what will be for me a transgressive experience.

What will it tell me about myself that I am presently unaware of?

If I model for Deborah and her life group I must offer myself to be gazed upon with total frankness. I'm not sure that I am brave enough to face the group without clothing.

Modelling nude, even just for Deborah, will be scary. It's the subtle differences that matter when life drawing. The shape of the eyes, ears, noses, hands, feet, are unique characteristics of each individual but naked differences extend to the sexual organs. And it's different for girls.

By choosing how she sits or stands, with her legs together or apart, a woman can expose, or avoid, a full display of her intimate femaleness. This not the case for a male. Even when flaccid, maleness protrudes. It sometimes gets hard, and even when not aroused is inclined to twitch, change size, or drip, particularly in a standing pose. Yet the discipline of life drawing insists the artist studies all details to understand the human mechanism. The physiology of each and every female is distinct and special, as is that of every male, but a male nude has to bare a particularly self-willed, part of himself. A woman model can keep her sexual feelings mysterious if she pleases.

How will I feel if my penis decides to offer a particularly intimate insight into my inner feelings, as it did with Dr Mercedes?

Artist Hugh Kilmer who has led workshops to train models and written a manual for new models, says 'Erections are not only possible for a male model. They are likely'. But he insists, 'a model must risk an involuntary erection to display what it means to be human: human both as strength, and as weakness. The revelation of self is the essence of modelling as an art.'

To model for Deborah will take me well outside my comfort zone. But it will give me a chance to experience the much vaunted spiritual dimension of life drawing, and its ability to offer a window into the reality of both the artist and the model.

Artists I have met whose drawing skills I admire have also modelled, their greater understanding of the emotion of the model seems to improve their drawing. Is this the next step for me to improve?

I risk making myself a figure of ridicule by exposing myself. Yet Deborah keeps telling me that to draw well and to create good art I need to open myself up to the risk of failure. Only then will I learn and improve.

If I show my naked self to her will my professional reputation diminish? Or will my honesty give her a deeper and richer appreciation of my human presence? Will it enhance her sense of the real me and give her insight into my soul?

Modelling is the greatest and potentially most rewarding adventure that art still has to offer me so I will try to pluck up the courage to ask Deborah if I may model nude for her. But becoming deliberately nude will compel me to face up to the human emotions and inhibitions which have shaped me and carried me through my life.

I am decided.

I will ask Deborah if she will permit me to stand naked before her. She didn't hide anything when she posed for me and looked into my eyes while I stared. I want to look in her eyes while she draws me and see if I feel nude and empowered, or naked and terrified.

After the next session, at which Joan modelled, I did approach Deborah and asked if she would draw me.

I had made sure that I would have to discuss the issue by sending her an email in advance saying that I wanted to model for her. She asked what I had in mind. At once I felt a rush of embarrassment about what I was about to ask. I could feel my face going red.

What I was effectively about to say was. 'If I take all my clothes off will you draw me naked.'

Put like that it sounds pervy. But if I wanted to find out what it's like to model in the nude for a serious artist this was my only chance. I took a deep breath, pretended I felt confident and started to explain.

'What I'd like to do is model nude for you,' I began, 'so that I can learn about the model's perspective.'

'It might not turn out as you expect.' She said. 'You might not like it. You might not even see as much as you expect.'

'I don't think I am ever going to fully understand life drawing unless I take the risk, and model as well as draw.' I said.

'Why don't you model for the group?' she said. 'That will give you the experience.'

'I don't have the nerve to do that,' I said. 'It's been difficult enough for me to ask you to let me pose for you.'

'You might be nervous at first but if you try it, you'll find it's easy.' She said. 'Whenever a model fails to turn up either Jack or I model for this group.'

'I know,' I said. 'It was seeing Jack unexpectedly undress and pose which gave me the idea. He managed to strike positions which were interesting to draw and his poses were so communicative. He made me realise that I might extend my understanding of the relationship between the artist and the model by posing. After seeing you having to push Jack to perform with no prior notice, I thought perhaps I should have offered to pose whilst clothed, but I was far too nervous to speak up. I didn't have the nerve to offer then and it wasn't until you posed nude for the group that I was able to work up the courage to offer to pose for you now.'

'Well,' she said. 'This is a safe space to pose for the first time. It's also a place to be yourself and be honest about who you are.'

'It's something I've wanted to try ever since I saw Jack do it,' I said, 'but until I also saw you do it I haven't dared to suggest it for fear of seeming ridiculous.'

'OK,' she said. 'I'll draw you nude. But can Maureen draw you too?'

I could see why she wanted Maureen there. I might be a harmless student of life drawing seeking to widen my experience, or I could be a sexual predator trying to set up an opportunity to attack her. By asking for another woman to be present she was testing if I really wanted the experience or was just trying out some strange sexual fetish.

'Of course she can,' I said immediately. 'And if it works out, I'll think about modelling for the group.'

'It will have to be in a few weeks' time,' she said. 'I've got a lot on at the moment.'

'That's fine.' I said. Inside I was elated that I had got agreement in principle and hadn't been laughed off as an oddball. I was secretly pleased she had asked for Maureen to be part of the session as it would make the experience more real.

I felt a rush of excitement at the thought that my naked body was to be the focus of attention for two female artists for a couple of hours. For some time I had wondered what it would feel like, soon I would know.

'Drop me an email and we'll sort out a time.' She said.

'I certainly will,' I said as I left.

The hardest thing had been asking her to draw me nude. Now all I had to do was fix the details then drop my robe for her to draw me.

Life drawing is an exercise in self-mastery and the careful management of desires and behaviours that in the outside world are regarded as sexual, rather than artistic or professional. I was going to take a risk and push my boundaries to experience the interaction between artist and model from the viewpoint of a naked model.

Deborah has inspired me to think about life drawing in a new way. I've moved from an emphasis on the figurative representation of the external appearance of human bodies towards wanting to capture the emotion of the encounter using the shape and energy of making marks. Deborah's understanding of drawing the human body had expanded to include capturing her model's emotions, movements, desires, reactions and her pictures communicate experiences, sensations and cravings shared between her and the model. I want to experience life drawing as she does. Her drawings come to life and capture the soul of the living model.

Picasso said, that the revelation of self is the essence of life modelling. I want to discover my real self, but whilst practising self-mastery of my own urges. When I study Deborah's drawing of me I will know exactly how her model felt as he was being drawn.

Over thousands of generations, humans have learned that showing off a naked body sends out sexual signals that threaten the security of mating pairs. Most of us have chosen to agree that that is a bad thing. Artists disagree. Now I will discover if I feel shame while I am closely scrutinised over an extended period without clothing to conceal my reactions.

Shame is the emotion that enforces the social code of wearing clothes in public. We try to avoid shame because it feels so unpleasant. How much shame will I experience during my nudity? Will I feel that I am a threat to the basic social fabric of society? I am choosing to expose my sexual self in a group context that gives every participant an opportunity for sexual behaviour outside of their principal unions.

In the quest to improve my drawing skills I have been consistently practicing unnatural behaviour, such as pretending I find nothing sexual in looking intently at a naked woman, or find nothing unusual about sitting with a group of clothed people in a circle around a naked individual.

The ritual of life drawing sets out to normalise what would otherwise be exhibitionist or voyeuristic behaviour. To experience how this set of rules functions I intend to observe how much of my emotional self I will project, and how I will feel about it, when I become the naked individual while the female artists follow the life room conventions.

For me to appear naked before female artists will be a reversal of the historic artistic tradition of a naked female submitting to the intense gaze of a group of clothed males.

The artist's gaze has traditionally mediated a power relationship far beyond natural visual curiosity. This intense scrutiny will take place in the setting of a studio, which is Deborah's home ground and I will be in the subordinate role. When I expose the private parts of my body, the potential for ridicule, humiliation and shame is tremendous. I will be offering an intimate revelation of myself.

I suspect there must always be a sense of disappointment when any man reveals the size and shape of his penis, no matter what he looks like. How will Deborah react? Will she even be interested? To me, my penis is not just any body part, it is the most important aspect of my masculinity. Flaunting it will render me susceptible to her critical evaluation.

I normally protect my manhood from casual appraisal by wearing clothing. I am to give up that protection. I can't help wondering what Deborah will think when she sees my body. She has warned me that the drawing she makes could be brutal in its assessment.

Do I really want to do this? Will this session be ethical and professional?

Among adults nudity is almost exclusively associated with sexual availability. Am I just providing sexual entertainment for two inquisitive spectators? The life studio normally functions as a controlled theatre of naked display and spectatorship but the sexual issue remains an inherent part of it. The artist's studio is traditionally a safe space for transgressive encounters where sexuality does not have to be pinned down, explained or isolated, but can move in and out of the feelings and desires of the participants.

I keep telling myself that my main aim is to develop my drawing skill, and understand the whole emotional context of life drawing. But it is the sexual and transgressive element of this venture which creates the sense of risk and excitement for me. And this risk is centred around exposing my penis and its behaviour whilst visible in what is intended to be a non-sexual context.

Whilst teaching me life drawing Deborah's approach has been to contain, sublimate and deny the presence of sexual interest in the studio. But this does not mean that there will not be a sexual dimension to this encounter. There is no way that I can pretend that posing naked for Deborah will not be a sexual experience for me. But it is not my main reason for wanting to do it.

I do want to understand the emotional dynamic between the artist and the model from both sides of the clothed and unclothed divide. By posing naked in a semi-public context I am pushing my professional envelope into an uncomfortable new area. It is only because I have retired that I feel I dare take the risk. I want the emotional and artistic insight that that this experience can give me. I will have to trust my penis not to humiliate me. The object of the exercise is to move beyond my comfort zone to learn about the sensual emotion of art. The price of this knowledge is making myself a sexual object and exposing my penis, along with the rest of my body, to the ascetic appraisal of Deborah and the drawing she makes.

I arranged the session for a time when I knew my wife would be away for a few days and I would be at home alone.

I didn't expect to be nervous about posing nude, but I was. At 3:00 am on the morning of the sitting I woke up, with a strong erection and remembered I was to pose for Deborah in about 15 hours' time. As I lay in bed, half asleep, I had doubts if I would have enough self-control not to be aroused during the sitting. I wondered if I ought to call it off as it had such potential to be embarrassing. I went back to sleep in a state of uncertainty about whether to go ahead.

Soon after 4:00 am I woke again. For a few moments I wasn't sure who I was or where I was, then I remembered what I was committed to do later that day and I realised I was hard again. I became more nervous that I was going to make a fool of myself in front of Deborah.

As the sitting drew nearer I was beginning to realise how exposed I was going to be. My body seemed intent on reminding me that I couldn't control it and if it wanted to have an erection it would do so. There was nothing my mind could do to stop it. I tried counting slowly to see if I could relax myself back to flaccidity but fell asleep before I had any effect. The next thing I knew I awoke at about 5:30 and I was hard again. I normally sleep through to the alarm clock at 7:30, a morning erection is usual and doesn't bother me but my nervousness about the nude modelling I had committed myself to, was preying on my mind. I started to plan what I should do if I did inadvertently get aroused whilst trying to pose but went back to sleep before I reached any conclusions, only to wake again, with an erection, at 6:30 am.

This time I did think though my choices. I decided there were two main options about how to act if I got an erection.

If Deborah said something I had two possible responses.

1. If she says to continue to pose, to just ignore it stay in pose and try to think of something to distract myself.

2. If she asks if I want to take a break, to ask her if she would prefer that or if she would rather keep drawing other parts of me while the distraction goes away of its own accord.

I should then do what she asks, either keep still until it goes down or take a break and put my robe on until it goes down.

But what if Deborah ignores it? My options are.

1. Ignore it as well and pretend it isn't happening.

2. Apologise and ask for a short break, put my robe on and hope it goes down quickly.

Thinking this though I realised it might be an embarrassment for me, but it will be less so for Deborah, as she has worked with inexperienced male models before. Making a fuss about an unplanned erection would be a nuisance and a disruption of her creative process. She has already told me that she needs to get into a transcendental state to draw and the purpose of the model is to act as focus for this. That takes time and when she achieves it she becomes highly engaged in her line making.

Spontaneous, non-sexually motivated arousal happens to males. It had happened to me four times that morning, probably instigated by nervousness at the way I was pushing my boundaries to learn, but it implied it could occur during the sitting.

If it doesn't then there is no issue. But if it does and I make a fuss about it then I will upset Deborah's drawing mood. If she is bothered she will say something. She knows I have never modelled nude before. If she says nothing then neither should I. I must stay still and quiet. If need be I can apologize after the sitting when she has finished drawing. That way I won't break her concentration.

Having decided on a plan of action I went back to sleep.

I had a shower when I got up, to make sure I was properly clean. I hoped to have time to shower again just before I had to set off for the session as I knew I would be busy all day and the weather would be hot. I was bound to get sweaty during the day. I didn't want to smell when I disrobed.

I returned home and showered again before I set off to Deborah's studio, aiming to arrive by six o'clock.

As I drove over to the studio, with each passing mile I got more nervous. The butterflies in my stomach were fluttering up a veritable storm of anticipation.

I parked outside the chapel, and my legs felt weak at the prospect of what I was committed to do. There was a seemingly endless stream of cars coming down the road and the longer I had to wait to get out, the more my fears grew. The butterflies in my tummy had been replaced by a flock of crows trying to peek their way out into the evening sunlight. At last the traffic thinned enough for me to open my car door. As I walked up to the big chapel door, I had a flashback to going there to Sunday

School as a child. Much childhood teaching about sin and the corruption of the flesh passed through my mind as I looked up at the chapel façade. All that preaching and what was I planning to do? I was about to spend two hours lolling about naked for the entertainment of two women, in the meeting hall of the establishment which had warned me I was destined to burn in Hell Fire if I didn't keep myself pure.

My elder self quickly reassured my Inner child that this old chapel was now an artist's studio and devoted to spiritual freedom rather than religious suppression. I took a deep breath to calm my jangling nerves, opened the door and stepped inside.

Deborah was there and so was Maureen. For about five minutes we stood and talked about drawing materials and the relative detachment of computer drawing tools as compared to paper, charcoal and paint. I suspect I was burbling and rambling on a little as I was wondering when they'd tell me to undress and how my disrobement would go. I was trying to put off that moment so I kept talking about nothing in particular. Finally Deborah managed to stop me burbling.

'You can get changed over there,' she said, pointing to the corner of the side room where I had once spied on Maureen as she undressed.

Maureen was setting up her easel and wasn't bothering about me. I moved to the side room, took off my watch and placed it in my trouser pocket. Next I took off my trousers, followed by my shirt. I put on my dressing gown, and removed my socks and underpants under its protection. I fastened the dressing gown about me and put on my slippers.

If Maureen was surreptitiously watching me then I hadn't repaid my first view of her with a flash of my own backside.

'Do you want a drink?' Deborah said as I appeared in my robe. As she spoke I suddenly felt an overwhelming pressure in my bladder. The tension of undressing and standing about in a flimsy gown was getting to me. The child inside me desperately needed a wee, and the adult managing my body had to do something about it before the moment to drop my robe arrived. The last thing I needed was an impromptu impersonation of the *Manneken Pis* pose to mark my first public appearance as a Nude.

'No thank you,' I said, 'but I really could do with visiting the loo. You have no idea just how nervous I am. You're certainly pushing me well beyond my comfort zone.'

'You'll soon get used to it' Deborah said, expressing a confidence which I didn't feel. I trusted her but I didn't believe her, however, once I'd relieved the pressure on my bladder I felt less stressed. I was committed and within a matter of seconds I was going to be naked in front of Maureen and Deborah. I took a few deep breaths and composed myself for the inevitable moment when I would have to drop my gown.

Then Deborah gave me an unexpected stay of execution.

'Keep your gown on for now,' Deborah said, 'while we sort out a pose.'

She asked me to sit on a lounger, sideways to her and with my back towards Maureen and make myself comfortable. She suggested various ways of sitting which I experimented with, until I found one I thought I could hold.

'Are you happy with that, Maureen?' she said.

'It's fine for me,' Maureen said. 'I like back views'.

'Do you think you can hold that position for ten minutes?' Deborah said to me.

'I think so,' I said.

'Ok,' she said. 'If you'd like to slip your gown off, then we'll try ten minutes.'

The moment I had been anticipating and rehearsing in my mind since I had first plucked up the courage to ask Deborah to draw me had finally arrived. I felt a strange mixture of anticipation and dread as I undid my belt, opened my gown and shrugged it off my shoulders. Now I was sitting on it, not wearing it. I had imagined I would have stood up for a dramatic dropping of the robe followed by an embarrassing and revealing struggle to get into position. But Deborah managed my transition from clothed to naked in such a simple and natural way my great reveal was an anti-climax.

Now I was sitting naked in front of Deborah and Maureen and I was terrified. Even though I had my legs close together, I was certain I was going to embarrass myself. Only when I saw their drawings afterwards, did I realise that neither of them could see my genitals.

'Say if you need to move,' Deborah said. 'Look up out of the window, and hold the pose for ten minutes.'

This was when I realised that modelling was quite different from what I expected. I was looking towards the window so I couldn't see what the women were doing.

People tell you that you should try to live your dreams. I was living the popular nightmare of standing naked in front of a packed lecture theatre, even if it was scaled down to a class of only two. I had nowhere to hide and felt completely exposed. All I was wearing was my personality and I was terrified of exposing myself as an embarrassing fool.

It was much harder to keep still than I expected. But what I had not foreseen was because I needed to keep my head still, I couldn't look around. My field of view was filled with the summer blue of the evening sky. Like Adam, I knew I was naked but I couldn't even look down to check if my body was behaving politely.

The studio was pleasantly warm and a slight breeze from the open window was wafting gently around my groin. The main sound was the scratching of brushes, charcoal or pencils on paper. In a different, fully clothed, world outside, cars drove by, the rising and falling of their doppler-shifted exhausts rhythmically reminding me I was no longer a part of their normality. I was not only naked I was being closely scrutinised and I had volunteered for this exposure.

The fears of my morning arousals flowed back into my mind. I had to stay in this vulnerable position for ten minutes. All I could think was that even though I was indecently exposed with my genitals being intimately caressed by a teasing zephyr, I must not become aroused. I had to control my fear and suppress unwanted reactions by diverting my mind to something other than the possibility of humiliating myself in front of Deborah and Maureen. I decided to count the seconds of the ten minutes. Slowly and remorselessly I counted. One and two and three and four. I added the 'ands' to make sure each count took a second. When I reached 'sixty and', I tagged a finger of my left hand by pressing it against my side.

I had progressively reached the stage of tensing a fifth finger on my other hand when I heard Deborah say 'Three more minutes.'

I kept counting, concentrating only on the progression of numbers.

'You can stretch now,' Deborah's voice said from somewhere in the far distance, and at that moment I realised that the muscles in my legs had become quite stiff. I stood up, leaving my robe on the lounger. I was focussed on the need to get my circulation moving again and I shamelessly stretched my legs, twisted my torso and arched my back. For the first time since I had slipped out of my robe I forgot I was naked.

'How did that feel?' Deborah asked. I turned to face her, pushing my elbows back and rolling my head around to free of my neck and shoulder muscles. 'Make sure you stretch all the tension away.' She said.

'It's holding my head still at an angle which has stiffened me most,' I said, while I rolled my shoulder blades, compressed and relaxed my stomach muscles whilst rotating my hips to free up my thigh muscles.

'It was interesting pose to try to capture,' Deborah said, 'your upper body was quite centred while your bottom half was a tangle of shapes.'

'It was good back view, and you kept very still,' I heard Maureen's voice say from behind me. 'The sidelight highlighted the detail of your spine.'

As I was talking and stretching my body to relieve the tension of posing I realised that I was making a total exhibition of myself. I was displaying everything I normally kept discreetly concealed in my trousers. Deborah seemed concerned that I hadn't over strained my muscles and was watching me carefully to make sure I was moving ok.

'You can move slightly during the pose to relieve any pressure on your body if you need to', she said. 'You're not just an inert manikin, you're supposed to be a living, breathing human that moves.'

I was having a civilised conversation about the mechanisms and limitations of posing whilst putting on a far more explicit display then ever happened in The Full Monty. And I wasn't concerned. It felt natural. I was naked, uninhibited and stretching freely, in front of Deborah and Maureen and nothing dreadful had happened. Even without the social armour of clothing I could still function as a civilised human being.

When I later looked at the drawing Deborah did, I can see the tension in my neck and my torso as I struggled to accept that I was naked for a clothed audience. My preoccupation with counting to distract myself from the fear of having an erection showed in the blankness of my eyes. The expression on my face looked strained and worried. And I was worried. I was fighting to remain calm in what was, for me, a novel and weird situation and I was afraid of losing control. But although I was worrying about the condition of my penis, neither of the women could see it. Neither my genitals or buttocks had been on show until the pose ended and I stood up to stretch.

I could have put on my robe to stretch but the thought never entered my head. Deborah had been right. I had quickly adapted to being naked in front of two clothed women artists.

'Are you ready to try another ten minute pose,' Deborah asked.

I shrugged my whole body to check I had no residual tension and nodded. Then as I looked down at myself, once again the reality that I was naked struck me, but this time I forced myself to spread my gown over the seat, as Deborah described the pose she wanted. I had removed my clothing and I wasn't going to retreat back into it. I had managed one ten minute pose without disaster, I could do it again.

'Can you look to your left?' Deborah said.

I glanced down to make sure I was flaccid and calm before I fixed my eyes on the far wall. As in the previous pose I could not see either Deborah, Maureen or myself.

My initial coyness was giving way to a feeling of amazement that I was allowed, no I was urged, to be naked and the centre of attention for two women. As I reflected on how I felt during the first pose my morning erection fears crept back into the worry corner of my mind. Whilst stretching and talking I had forgotten how exposed I was. Now as I sat staring at the wall my sense of amazement at the novelty of being still, quiet and naked began to give way to worries about the embarrassment of inadvertent arousal. The gentle breeze was still caressing me, I was more relaxed than last time, but my knees were further apart and subjectively I felt my groin was more visible (although when I saw the drawings later I realised that once again they couldn't see my genitals). But I didn't know that at the time so I continued to worry. Rather than counting I decided to try a slow breathing meditation to focus my mind on something other than the turbidity of my penis.

The method I used was to breathe in for a count of eight, hold my breath for a count of four, breathe

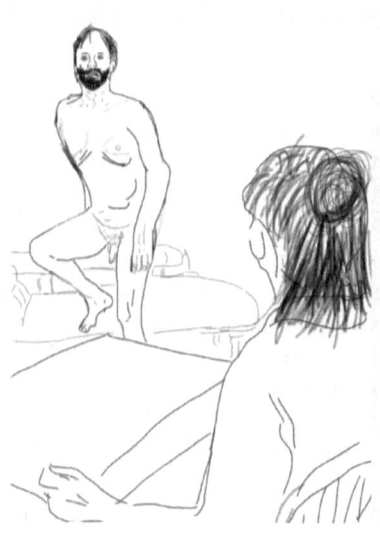

out for a count of eight and then wait for a further count of four before starting the whole cycle again. This focus on breathing is a relaxing form of meditation and when combined with the gentle feel of the air moving around my body I soon lost myself in mindfulness of the present.

I was surprised when Deborah told me there were only three minutes left to pose and I felt almost annoyed at being disturbed. I hadn't noticed the time passing and I quickly fell back into the meditative rhythm of breathing.

'You can stretch now.' Deborah said, roughly dragging me back from my mindscape into the real world. I shook my head to stop the automatic breathing routine and stood up to stretch.

'That was much easier.' I said. I was happy to chat as I went through another full frontal display of muscle relief, without even thinking about what I was showing.

When I looked at Deborah's sketch, later, I could see I was far more relaxed than I had been during the first pose and she had captured the blankness of my face as I drifted through the mental world of being aware of myself. It is interesting to see how Deborah saw me as I mediated. I looked calm, centred but mentally distant in that drawing.

'How do you feel about trying a standing pose?' Deborah said.

'Why not?' I said.

I was feeling much more confident now. I stood with my legs apart. My left foot pointing towards Deborah with my right foot at a

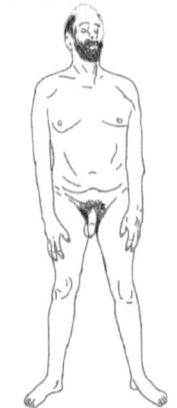

forty-five degrees to my body. I put my arms by my side, I was sideways on for Maureen.

'How's that?' I said.

'That's fine,' Deborah said. 'Let's try ten minutes. If you feel dizzy at all, then sit down. A standing pose is much harder than a seated one.'

How right she was. Less than an hour after first slipping shyly out of my robe I was now standing in front of Deborah and Maureen with my legs apart and my arms at my side. There was nothing modest or retiring about this pose. I was certainly becoming more comfortable in the nude.

'Can you look to your right,' Deborah said.

I looked to my right and found I was looking straight into the calm brown depths of Maureen's eyes. She winked at me.

'That's fine.' Deborah confirmed so I settled down to watch Maureen's eyes as she drew me.

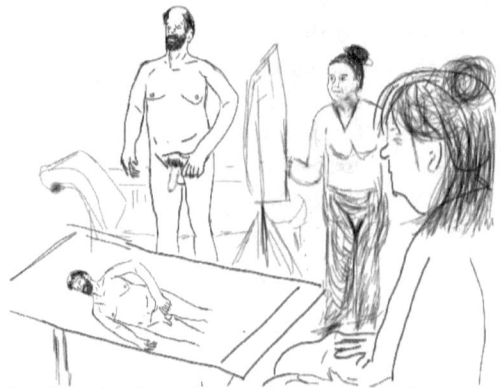

She kept looking directly into my eyes but without making eye contact with me. It was only when I looked at her drawing that I found she was drawing my face. The position of my feet made standing quite comfortable and I didn't have much of a problem holding the pose for ten minutes. And I stopped worrying about spontaneous erections. I just kept watching Maureen's cold intrusive eyes as she drew me.

Deborah's drawing showed the back of my head merging into the background. The impression it creates is that I live more in my head than in my body and as a result my head is merging into the world and my body is simply supporting my thoughts. The ten minutes passed quickly. Strangely Deborah's drawing seems to have captured my worry that my revealed body was more important that my head and I was more concerned about my nudity than posing my face and head.

'You can put your robe on and take a break,' Deborah said.

I put on my dressing gown and slippers then had a look at the drawings. Deborah had done a full frontal figure but Maureen had drawn a head portrait. I felt somehow disappointed that having made the effort to expose everything she simply drew the face I always display. It had been quite an act courage to reveal my body as fully as I had. While we stood and drank cups of tea I had a discussion with Maureen

'Why did you only draw my face, when I was forcing myself to reveal my whole body?' I said.

'Because your face showed just how exposed you felt.' She said. 'You're normally so reserved and controlled but when you were naked your facial expression was more human and vulnerable than I had ever seen you look before.'

'I have never felt so exposed and humble as I did when you kept staring into my eyes without making any human contact.' I said.

'A model has to learn not to expect human contact from an artist,' Maureen said. 'The hard stare goes with the territory.'

I was naked beneath my flimsy gown which gaped open when I leaned forward, but I could have been holding a polite philosophical conversation in the senior common room with any woman colleague. I was certainly becoming more at ease without clothing.

Deborah meanwhile was setting up a couch and a lamp ready for the next pose which was to be a seated one.

'Just sit comfortably on the couch, ' Deborah said.

I took off my robe, placed it on the chair and sat down on it. The couch was facing Deborah's easel.

'Just relax your legs.' She said.

I did as I was told. Deborah told me to look to my left so I found a spot on the wall to focus on. This was a very open pose with my genitals fully exposed. By now I was not worried about what the women might see, I simply looked at the studio wall where a mirror was reflecting the windows making a triangular shape. As I sat I started to visualise the Platonic shapes in 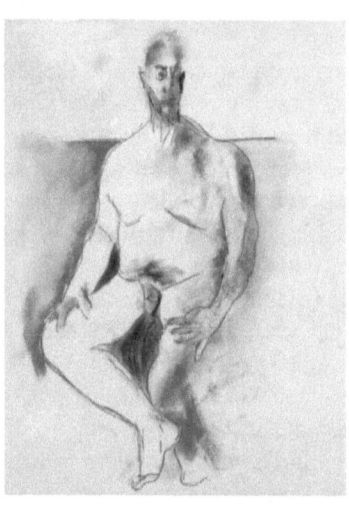 sequence carefully visualising each perfect pattern in turn. The pose passed quickly and I was surprised when Deborah told me I had held it for twenty minutes.

When I looked at Deborah's drawing later I saw she had portrayed me in a heroic mould. I thought I looked like a drawing of Plato. This really did surprise me as I had not told Deborah I was thinking about Platonic forms as she drew me.

Once I had stretched and restored my circulation Deborah pulled a couch out. 'Let's finish the session with a reclining pose,' she said.

I spread my robe on the lounger and lay down on my side facing away from her.

'That's not working,' she said. 'Lie flat on your back, with your legs up. Can you put your hands behind you head,' I did as she asked and realised I was lying with my legs spread and my genitals exposed to the breeze and fully visible to both Deborah and Maureen.

'Now tilt your head and look this way.' She said. I did and realised this was a pose where I would be able to see Deborah as she drew me.

I watched Deborah's eyes and hands as she drew me and I was intrigued by the process, which seemed to involve quite a bit of studied observation and sighting, followed by bursts of mark making activity, during which she was continually looking from the paper to me and making adjustments. Looking at that drawing later I could see the intensity of my curiosity in my face and I look

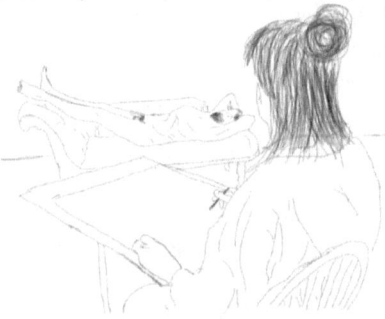

frighteningly intense, much more than I had ever realised consciously. In that final pose I felt vulnerable and very much the junior in the artistic partnership as Deborah drew me.

But as I had eye contact I couldn't stop myself talking to her. I was wondering if I was fulfilling her expectations in the pose, so I asked her if she wanted me to move. I only kept quiet once she explained that she was analysing the pose before she started drawing. From then on I shut up and concentrated on watching what she did. She certainly captured my intense interest in the process of making that drawing.

This pose also passed quickly and when it ended Deborah told me I could get dressed. My brief time as the centre of attention was over.

I finished the session on an emotional high and as I stretched my naked body in front of the two woman I asked if I could model for them again later in the week.

'I was much more relaxed as the session went on. ' I said. 'But I think I could do a better job of modelling if I tried again as I won't be so nervous. I could make the same time on Thursday, if you two could. How about it?'

'I'm ok, ' Maureen said. 'As long as you are Debby.'

Deborah shrugged her shoulders 'Why not?' she said.

'Thank you,' I said and bowed, forgetting I was still nude.

'Time to get dressed Maurice,' Deborah said, handing me my gown. She was most careful to give me privacy while I dressed and Maureen left as soon as she had packed her drawing kit.

I drove home is a state of high elation. I had done it. I had modelled nude for two clothed women and I had not embarrassed either myself or them. What's more I was going to repeat the performance later that week. And I wasn't the least nervous. Instead I was looking forward to it. Now I understood what Kathleen Rooney meant when she had written.

'Nudity is an essential element to artistic development. Though many people find public nudity taboo; real artists find it perfectly acceptable, even enjoyable.'

As a model I had socially progressed to a position where being naked in front of others was easy. I had imagined that the first occasion I had to drop my robe in front of strangers would be the most difficult but Deborah had made it an easy transition for me.

Nude is nude, whether sitting down or standing up. I couldn't be any more nude once I had slipped my robe off and by the end of the session I stood up and moved about without reluctance.

I had been nude voluntarily and enjoyed the modelling experience, so much that I intended to repeat it.

Chapter 12 Joining the Social Theatre

The life-room is a form of social theatre, where controlled spectatorship is structured around a performance by a still, silent, naked model. One of the interesting factors, peculiar to life-drawing classes, is the movements between artists and models, and the fact that a significant number of life-drawing participants spend time on both sides of the easel. This makes life-drawing distinct from other practices of bodily display or performance (such as sex-entertainment), and supports the idea that life-drawing is better understood as a collaborative performance by a collection of interchangeable role players.
-Margaret Mayhew

I was not nervous before my second nude session with Deborah and Maureen. I showered and deodorized to make sure I was intimately clean and set off in plenty of time. I took the bag, containing my robe and slippers, from the car and went in. Deborah was preparing the studio. Maureen had not yet arrived.

We talked for a few minutes about what I had learned from the previous session and I asked how she had so accurately interpreted what I was thinking in her drawings. She said she didn't know, she just drew what she felt and reacted to the emotions she felt during the encounter.

'Should I get ready?' I said. 'Or should I wait for Maureen?'

'Go ahead and change,' Deborah said. I went to the loo to make sure I wasn't going to be stressed about needing to urinate whilst naked. When I returned to the studio Deborah and Maureen were moving some stuff about in the side room, where I had changed the previous week. I reasoned that as they had both already seen me naked I may as well just undress in a corner of main studio. This time I didn't bother

211

changing beneath my robe. I simply stripped totally and folded my clothes before taking the robe from my bag and putting it on. As I did so I realised that this was exactly what I had watched Maureen do when I spied on her getting changed. By the time I was ready Deborah had finished arranging props.

'You can put your things in there,' Deborah said, looking disapprovingly at my discarded clothes and pointing to the side room. I did as I was told. When I returned, she was sitting at an easel and arranging her drawing paper and charcoal. Maureen had set up an easel too.

'Will you sit on the couch with your arm over the back?' she said. I doffed my gown, without any fuss, laid it on the chaise lounge and sat down in the pose she asked for. By now I was wholly comfortable being naked in front of the women. Deborah looked at me for a minute or so, and then asked me to get up while she moved the couch further along into the evening sunlight. I stood to the side but didn't put on my gown. Once she was satisfied with the way the light was falling on the couch, she told me to sit back down.

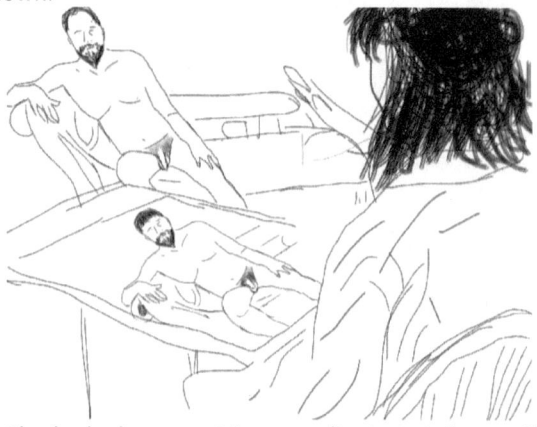

She looked over at Maureen. 'Is that ok for you?' she said. Maureen nodded her approval. As they were both satisfied with the pose they started to draw.

I was sitting facing Deborah with my legs apart, I had my right arm on the end of the chaise lounge and my left arm on my knee. This pose made my genitals fully visible as I was facing Deborah and my knees were wide apart, so much so that my legs were at an angle about seventy-five degrees.

By the time I was ten minutes into the pose the side of my foot started to hurt. The whole weight of my leg was resting on a strip of flesh about a quarter of an inch wide and I had to flex the foot slightly to avoid it going to sleep. I had stopped worrying about having an erection and was more concerned about keeping still and thinking idealistic thoughts to keep my body language heroic, rather than terrified. This time I was confident I could control myself.

I was much more comfortable being nude and wasn't bothered about how much of me the artists could see.

The pose lasted for 18 minutes but it seemed to pass very quickly. When it finished I stood up and stretched without any sense of embarrassment. I stood in front of the women, shaking my legs and discussing the next pose, without any feeling of self-consciousness.

'It might be wise now to get your feet up,' Deborah said. 'If you could lie down with your head at the low end of the couch with your feet up. If you need a pillow under your neck or your back tell me. Just try it and see how you feel'.

I put my arms behind my head to cradle my neck

'I'm a bit worried about your hands being that high up,' she said.

'I don't know how long I can hold this,' I said. I could feel a rather pleasant pull on my stomach muscles and I was a little worried the tension of stretching my belly while breathing might stimulate

213

my groin and arouse me. I didn't want to get an erection.

'Shall we just see how you manage?' Deborah said, as if reading my mind. 'Stretch if you need to then go back into the pose. Let's try ten minutes to see what happens.'

It was a comfortable and easy pose which pulled my stomach flat. I could feel my genitals tightening as each breath tensed my diaphragm. As I settled into pose, I was aware of my penis flopping about as I arched my back to get comfortable, but I knew I mustn't handle it into a more comfy position. This was a major difference from the medical nudity where I could handle my genitals and adjust their position. Under life room rules that was definitely forbidden. As I couldn't see my penis I had to let gravity do its thing and simply jiggle about until I felt settled. However, I remained intensely mindful of my penis moving slowly in time with my breathing.

I glanced sideways and saw Deborah spend a few minutes staring intently at my body before she made any move to put charcoal to paper.

Once she started drawing I relaxed and enjoyed the physical sensations. I stared upwards at the blank ceiling and listened to the scratching scrape of charcoal. I felt myself drifting into the quiet stillness of the pose. I was enjoying an absolute awareness of my skin. I imagined I could feel the touch of the artist's eyes darting over its surface, like a pair of pond skaters. I felt the hairs on my lower belly tingle as they felt stared at with great intensity. I sensed my stomach pulling tight and enjoyed the slow tensing and relaxing of the muscles of my abdomen, tugging gently at my groin, as I breathed. I stopped worrying and enjoyed the feeling of having my body teased by the tender caress of the slow moving air of the studio.

I only seemed to have been in pose for few minutes when Deborah stopped drawing and said, 'OK'.

I looked at the clock and saw that the pose has lasted 22 minutes. When I sat up I found that my hands were numb.

'That was very restful,' I said, 'except for my fingers.'

I didn't mention that it had also been erotic. The slow breathing movement of my lower body, the warm caress of the summer zephyr from the open window and the knowledge that I was being closely looked at by two women artists who I could hear scratching charcoal over the rough paper as they drew me had all combined into a delightful feeling of being a shameless centre of attention

'Mmm?' Deborah said, 'I noticed you enjoyed it,' smiling at me with a sort of knowing look.

I sat up and stretched my hands and fingers. I noticed Deborah was staring at me sitting with my legs apart, facing her. By now I was comfortable in my nakedness, but at that moment I realised that as soon as I came out of pose I was no longer a nude model. Now I was a naked man having an intimate conversation with a woman I hardly knew.

'You might need to get up and walk about,' she said. She didn't tell me to put my robe on, and I didn't think to. I stood up, stretched and walked to and fro in front of them both.

'What do you want to try next?' she said as I jiggled and gyrated in front of her.

'I'd like to try the classic Michelangelo pose of David.' I said.

She got up and walked towards me. I was surprised how close she came to me while I was naked. She didn't seem to be bothered about observing any model's zone of privacy. As she passed within a few inches of me I could feel her bow wave of displaced air moving over my skin. She picked up a high backed stool which she carried towards where I was standing.

'You might need some support for that pose.' She said and brought the stool towards where I stood. Again she walked within an inch or so of me. She was so close that I could feel the radiated heat of her body as well as the touch of the air her movement displaced. The breeze she trailed wafted over my genitals as she squeezed by. It was a surreal moment. I had not realised how sensitive my exposed skin would be to the air currents and radiated body heat of other people moving close to me. It was a tremendous insight into just how my clothes not only conceal bodily arousal but also restrict the sensations I might otherwise experience.

Deborah stood beside me and tried out the pose herself, using the stool to support her arms, she was checking how much strain there would be on my muscles. I mirrored her movements as she explored the pose. It was another surreal moment as I echoed her dressed body language, with my naked body. She dropped her hands to her groin and I mirrored her movements without thinking. As I brushed my genitals I suddenly realised that I had to keep my hands either at my sides or above my waist, as otherwise I was in danger of looking as if I was touching myself sexually. There are ways a male can place his hands when he is wearing clothes which become potentially lewd if he is naked.

'I was just wondering if that would be helpful?' she said looking at the stool, 'Can you use it as a support in some way.'

I moved towards her and stood by the stool, resting my arm on it.

'I don't think I can use it,' I said. 'David had a white stone in his left hand and a sling slung over his shoulder which he was holding in his right hand. If I copy the pose I don't have a spare hand to use the stool.'

I took the belt from my dressing gown to use as a sling. I had brought a white stone to hold, and I bent over to get it from my bag from where it lay on the floor close by Deborah's feet.

Now I was ready. I tried the pose, with the sling over my right shoulder, held in my right hand and my left arm dangling by my side, holding the stone.

'You look quite ready to go out and do battle with a giant,' Maureen said, 'I like the white stone.'

'I'm going to tell myself the story of David and Goliath while I pose,' I said. 'To get my body language right.'

'You do that,' Deborah said as I settled into my David pose. She watched me for a moment or two and then said. 'Are you comfortable?'

'Yes,' I said.

'If you feel dizzy or faint, then just sit down and relax,' she said and began to draw.

The pose lasted 22 minutes. The warm evening sun was shining more strongly through the side window of the studio on my left side. This was another revealing pose. My legs were apart, and I was facing Deborah with my genitals side-lit by the spotlight of a sun beam. Because I had my head slightly bowed I could glance down and could see the magnified shadow of my penis waving softly over my thigh like a sort of floppy sun dial. It was a bizarre feeling to stand with my body highlighted by the bright evening sun with my every twitch and sway magnified in a sort of shadow-puppet show. I could hide nothing. The sun was so warm I could feel myself beginning to perspire slightly. I was glad when its brightness was obscured by a cloud for the last ten minutes of the pose.

'Are you ok,' Deborah said to Maureen, as she finished drawing.

'Yes, that's fine, ' she replied.

'Have a stretch,' Deborah said to me.

As I was stretching and restoring my circulation Deborah got up and passed close to me again. Even though she did not actually touch me, my exposed skin felt her presence as a mix of warm moving air and a wash of radiant body heat. Had I been clothed I might not have worried that she was standing so near, but in my naked state she felt intimately close. I knew I'd been sweating slightly and without clothes to mask me, she was close enough to smell the fresh sweat off my skin. Sensing the air she displaced brushing my skin felt just as strange as it had previously, but this time I realised that as she was moving the air about she must also be able to smell my perspiration. Perhaps she did, but she didn't let on. She moved the stool into the centre of the floor and stood beside it, supporting herself with her hands on it and her back to the easel.

'How about a back view?' She said, 'Try this', demonstrating an upright pose. I moved close to her and stood as she did.

'Ok,' she said. 'If you're happy we'll go with this.'

There was a full length mirror on a stand in the corner of the studio and this pose had the advantage that I could see everything that was going on. The mirror was angled such that could see my own front view and Deborah on the right side of my reflection and also Maureen on the left. I was able to watch how they sighted, measured, stared and made lines.

The room was pleasantly warm as I stood leaning lightly on the stool to support the pose. I was enjoying watching what was happening. I was free to move my eyes, as the artists were drawing my back.

They both spent much more time looking than they did drawing. I soon got over the novelty of seeing my naked body standing in front of the woman artists and became engrossed in watching the intensity of their gaze. I eased the tension in my legs by moving them slightly wider apart and watched Maureen sight with her brush and adjust her drawing. She was closely scrutinising my backside but she wasn't perving because I had agreed to be naked and stared at.

I was getting comfortable in my skin. I was no longer worrying about how much of it the artists could see. Now I had removed my clothes there was nothing more to show. Or so I thought.

Then I realised that in the summer heat of the studio I was beginning to sweat more and more. I could feel the perspiration slowly oozing from my arm pits. I felt a droplet form and start to run down my side. This was not an totally novel feeling as it had often happened when I have been shirtless in the sun. But this was different. I felt a weird new sensation. When I have experienced sweat running

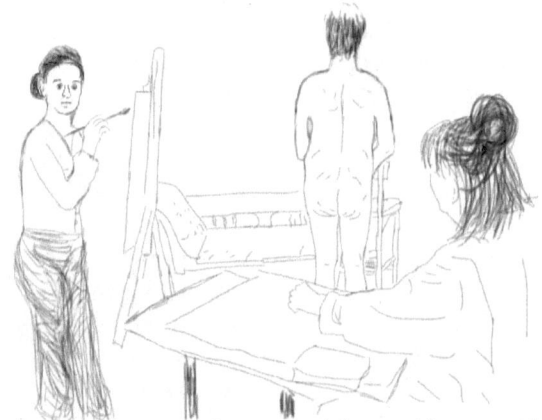

down from my underarms while working outside without a shirt, the tracing of the feathery finger-tips of the fluid secretions stopped at the waist band of my trousers. In the studio I wasn't wearing anything to stop the flow and I felt it continue across my thigh and down my leg. It felt is if I was being lightly caressed by a gentle feather from my arms down to my feet. I expected the sweat bead to stop at my waist. This one did not. I felt it trickle down my side, across my hip and down my leg to the floor.

Then it got worse. I felt a trickle of sweat start down my spine from around my shoulder blades. It was like the tender caress of a lover running a finger down my spine and with no waist band to stop it the caress followed the centre line of my buttocks and down my inside leg.

Both woman must have seen it, and yet the role of model obliged me to keep still. This was worse than getting an erection. They could see me sweat and watch the perspiration flow down my body. They must have been thinking how gross it looked. I could feel my face blushing and a quick glance in the mirror confirmed I was quite red. I hoped the flush hadn't spread to the back of my neck. Finally I understood just how revealing nudity can be when your spectators are up close.

Deborah must have noticed my embarrassment as she said. 'I take it you're warm enough?' In the mirror I could see a twinkle in her eye.

'Quite warm enough,' I said. 'Thank you.'

The slow caress of my own sweat droplets was an incredibly erotic feeling. I was glad I had my back to the artists. I concentrated on the pose and keeping still as the surface tension of the perspiration kept springing little mischievous surprises on my exposed skin. For a few minutes while the sun was at its strongest it was like a game of tickle and tease. Fortunately the sun dropped slightly in the sky, the room cooled a little and the water torture ceased as quickly as it had begun. Keeping totally still during this peculiar experience emphasised just how responsive my unclothed skin was to my environment.

We were about forty minutes into the pose when, in the mirror, I saw Deborah stand up and walk over to Maureen to look at what she was doing. I kept perfectly still, even though I felt her swirling the air around me. I realised then that I actually lived in a moving fluid, something my clothes usually stopped me noticing. I felt, rather than saw, her go back passed me before she reappeared in the mirror at her easel. She added a few final touches. Her easel made a scraping noise on the floor as she pushed it away.

'Ok, thank you very much,' she said. 'That will do, you can relax,'

I turned to face her.

'I managed over half an hour, ' I said.

'So you did,' she agreed.

Maureen stood up and brought her drawing over for me to see.

'You did really well keeping so still when you started to sweat.' She said. 'It really does tickle and annoy when it happens. The first time I felt it happening to me in pose, I was mortified.'

'I thought ladies didn't sweat they only glowed.' I said, grinning at her.

'It's been so hot this evening that I've been sweating all the time,' she said. 'But you couldn't see it because it happened under my clothes.' She lifted her arms and showed damp patches under the armpits. 'Well done, Maurice, you're well on the way to becoming a good model. You'll have to join the modelling rota for the group.'

I glowed with pleasure as I put on my gown.

Modelling has let me experience the form and function of the human body, without objectifying, sexualizing or clothing it. I could now appreciate how truly amazing naked bodies are. Posing in the birthday suit, that I started my life with, was an amazing thing. I had felt connected to the world and its atmosphere in ways a clothed person didn't notice. I had increased my awareness of myself, in a positive way and proved what a truly amazing thing the human form is.

I had been much more comfortable being naked during this second sitting and I felt an even greater exaltation of spirit as I drove home afterwards.

Chapter 13 Avoiding the Teapot of Doom

A nude model needs to have a mixture of confidence and indifference to be able to drop their robe in a room of clothed artists. The confidence gained by this work will only strengthen your personality. However, working as a nude model puts both the model and the artists in a vulnerable position. The model, is of course nude, and is at an automatic social disadvantage. This social disadvantage requires an extremely high degree of professionalism that must be maintained by both model and artist.

Eric Johnson and Suzette Roberts

Is there a moral to be drawn from my exploration of life drawing? Perhaps.

I have learned that I can be naked in a semi-public context without humiliating myself, without making a fool of myself and without having an involuntary exhibitionist erection.

I have found that is not necessary for me to speak or even make eye contact to communicate my feelings, my naked body can create a context from which Deborah and Maureen can capture an explanatory image.

I have been far more worried about showing my genitals and my physical reactions than either Deborah or Maureen have been about seeing them. In my first naked pose I was terrified that if I stopped counting the seconds I might lose control but neither Deborah or Maureen could see my penis from their viewpoints. The fear was in my mind, not in the situation. Only by doing something that challenged my comfort boundaries was I able to learn that nudity was not the terrifying issue I had feared.

I have learned that keeping still and quiet is easier when I do not have eye contact with the artist.

When I make eye contact I have a strong urge to speak.

I realised that what I was thinking as I posed affected the marks that the artists made and their images somehow tapped into how I felt rather that what I hoped to project.

I have concluded that life drawing is a powerful way of experiencing and communicating deep felt human emotions. My naked body couldn't help revealing what I was feeling to the insight of Deborah and Maureen's line making. I now understand that I cannot hide my thoughts and emotions if I am naked.

I didn't learn as much about drawing as I did about modelling. I had expected to see more of the drawing process than I did. With hindsight I now realise that I had forgotten just how different the model's viewpoint is from either the artist, or an impartial onlooker to the scene. The model's viewpoint is fixed by the pose and cannot be changed at whim.

Nude modelling is sensual. The pose when I tried breath mediation while feeling the movement of the warm summer air over my whole body felt sublime. I sensed my own breathing as part of the breath of the world. It was a novel experience to attempt that form of meditation whilst naked in public with warm summer air caressing my body. But I also noticed, when looking at Deborah's drawing, that withdrawal into my inner feelings resulted in a remote image. I just wasn't present in the pose.

What I think about while I pose matters a great deal. If I withdraw into a sensual meditative state I am too passive to create an inspiring image. If I worry about accidental sexual exhibitionism my tension shows. If I take too great an interest in what the artist is doing, or staring at, I look too detached, too critical, or too intense. If I enjoy the sensual eroticism of a pose my preoccupation with my sensations makes me appear introverted. But if I ponder philosophical thoughts I project calmness and serenity.

In the standing pose when I was watching Maureen, who unknown to me was drawing only my face, Deborah's drawing of my figure has captured the trepidation I was feeling. Although revealing my body was a big decision for me and really tested my will power, showing my head was unimportant. Maureen had noticed all the tension that showed in my face. That was why she did a portrait of only my face and head, even though I was exposing my entire body.

Deborah's life drawing studio and her groups of interchangeable artists and models has proved a safe place for me to facilitate a series of experiential encounters with reality. I have been successfully wafted away from the tempting strawberry jam of indolence to chase the elusive damsel flies of reality. I can see the shadow of the teapot of doom shrinking into insignificance.

When I posed for Deborah and Maureen I closed the final link in a triangular encounter where we had each played the role of Subject, Object and Reality. We had all contributed to a series of events of realism which had explored the gaps between subject and object, subject and subject, reality and representation. We were all participants in a problematic and compelling interaction of voyeurism, exhibitionism and spectatorship within a context of naked realism, stillness and presence.

We collectively moved beyond a one-sided relationship where only the artist makes a representation of the model, to a place of strange otherness, where we took turns to be naked, exhibitionist and artistically erotic.

Whilst in pose we were an object, whilst moving we were an example of naked honesty and whilst drawing we participated in the shared humanity of the nude body of the model.

When we moved between poses we regressed into a naked imperfect creature but in pose we became a perfect Artistic Object.

I have now experienced life drawing as a temporal, spatial and social practice.

As the artist I was a spectator to the naked performance of the model; whilst the model was moving between poses I was the voyeur of an undressed human; and as a model I enjoyed the deep pleasure of uninhibited exhibitionism.

I have journeyed into transgressivism and crossed the boundary of what is normally legitimate for a retired mathematics professor. I have explored an ambiguous entangled area of voyeuristic, sexual, artistic and emotional relationships.

Now I know why artists are so driven to draw the human body. It is because we all have a body of our own, and we know the look and feel of it, outside and in. This gives us an innate interest in other people's bodies. Our physical and emotional survival is finely tuned to the visual shapes, the proportions and the messages that other people's bodies convey. Bodies intrigue us, and naked bodies are the ultimate fascination. We know instinctively if a drawing of a nude looks right, and therefore we get instant feedback.

Life drawing is rewarding because the diversity of poses and shapes a naked human body generates offer endless novelty. Drawing these manifold shapes is a skill where I can always improve, it is a journey which is never spoiled by arrival. It acts as a great unblocking process because the model is physically present for a limited period (unlike a still-life arrangement) so there is little time to worry about the outcome, and a strong impulse to experience the now and get on with drawing. Life drawing holds both artist and model intensely in the present and makes us both aware of the joy of being alive.

Drawing a naked human is an absorbing engagement because the dynamics of the process are mutually active participation. Anyone is interesting to draw, so once we start to draw from life, we see people differently. Life drawing gives us a window into both our own and our model's souls. Just as the model experiences what it is like to expose, display and be observed intensely, so the artist is also laid bare - every error, every inadequacy of perception is permanently preserved on the drawing paper. Life drawing is something that many are afraid to risk trying, because they fear it is viewed by society as a weird pursuit. I faced that fear, admitted I was weird too and as a result learned a great deal.

To speak to human souls, Art needs to work through human souls. We resonate with, respond to and seek contact with Art which shares our longings, our suffering and our joy at beauty. To draw well and to create good art we need to open ourselves up to the risk of failure. Only then do we learn and improve. Life drawing both as an artist and as a model is the greatest and most potentially rewarding risk we can take in Art.

By participating in the social theatre of life drawing in all its aspects I made a choice to risk failure and ridicule. In consequence I have emerged as a truly Naked Draftsman.

I have been the observer, the artist and finally the model. By so doing I have come to better understand

227

the world I live in and found a new focus and joy in life.

Now I know, to be able to draw from life, you must first learn to love life.

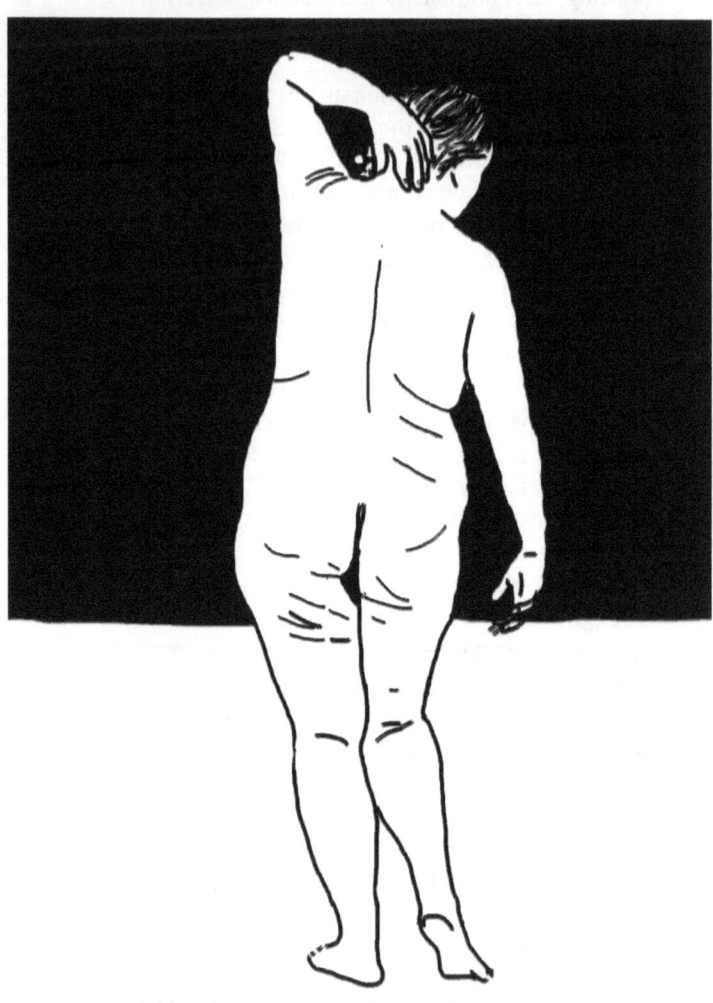